Praise for *Teenag*

"Teens are constantly barraged by peer pressure and media glamorization of immoral behavior. *Teenage Construction Zone* challenges them to examine their life foundation and realize that today's choices are tomorrow's consequences."

- Al Denson, Dove Award Winner, radio host, author, and philanthropist

"This book drives teenagers to recognize, examine, and deal with the key decisions they face growing up in the world today. Every student and parent should read this book... After all, the decisions our students make now will determine who they will be in the future."

- Jack Graham, Prestonwood

"My friend Trey Talley typically tears apart everything from telephone books to concrete blocks and baseball bats. In this book, he doesn't tell you how to tear things apart; he tells you how to keep your life together. The wisdom in these pages can help you to construct the firmest possible foundations for your life's dreams!"

- Dr. Timothy Paul Jones, Professor of Leadership, Bestselling author of more than a dozen books

"*Teenage Construction Zone* is a wonderful guide to help teenagers along the road of life. Not only will it greatly benefit you, but by applying it to your life, you'll be better equipped to help others."

- Dr. David Uth, FBC Orlando

"Foundations, so simple, yet so tough to build. Trey Talley gives the reader direction to some of the most important issues concerning life. *Teenage Construction Zone* is a must read for any youth who wants to build a solid footing for life."

- Guy Earle, President of Think Twice Ministries, former NFL player

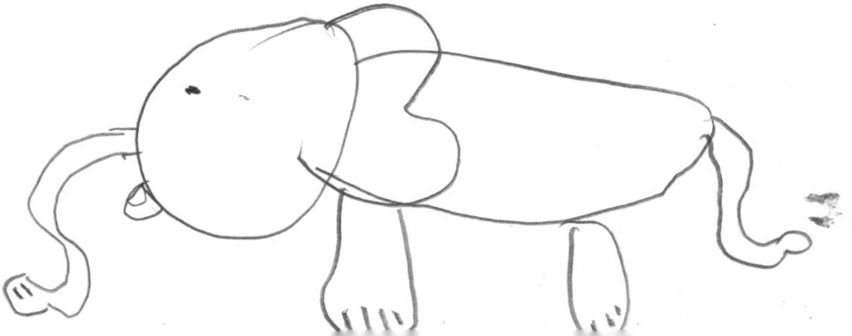

Praise for *Teenage Construction Zone*:

"Trey is a emphatic creative leader! He is a man with a passion to inspire and challenge those around him to achieve the most that life has to offer. *Teenage Construction Zone* is a perfect expression of his deep desire for young people to create a life with no regrets."
- Brandon Hensley, President of Team Impact

"Trey does a phenomenal job of tackling the key issues in a teenager's life using Biblical principles that are applicable, practical and relevant. From the foundation to the final product, this book presents a guideline for living that I highly recommend to anyone who is a teenager, has a teenager, or works with teenagers!"
- Jordan L. Easley, Second Baptist Houston

"As an educator for 27 years, I have witnessed countless teenagers building or tearing down their futures one choice at a time. Trey's book is a wonderful way to encourage positive construction. It reinforces why their decisions are important and encourages them to do some very serious thinking. *Teenage Construction Zone* is a tool that will benefit all who use it."
- Libby White, Middle School Principal

"Interesting, practical and clear, this book on the issues with which teenagers struggle, is a helpful tool for parents, youth workers, and teachers. And it is a book that your teenager will read, as well. Teenage Construction Zone will become a valuable resource for all who use it."
- Dr. Emil Turner, Ph.D., Executive Director of the Arkansas Baptist State Convention

"This is one motivating book! It lets teenagers know that they are in control of their lives. What they do with that power determines the life they will have. This book should be given to every teenager in our public schools. The message it carries is that important."
- Pat Allen, President, Clark County Retired Teachers Association

Praise for *Teenage Construction Zone*:

"TeenageConstruction Zone puts forth compelling truths that motivate young people to think deeply about the choices they are making. The book gives young people a clear moral compass to follow as they navigate through their formative years. It deals with problems that face teenagers and provides realistic answers."
Kevin Millwood, Texas Rangers Pitcher

"Like the man who built his house on the sand, many people are building life on a foundation that will ultimately fail. I believe youth and youth leaders who want to build a solid life from the ground up will gain valuable insight from Trey Talley's Teenage Construction Zone."
Jerry Cox, Executive Director; Arkansas Family Council

"As a Pastor I have tried to teach my people and especially my youth the importance of making right choices. Taking responsibility for your actions is lacking in our culture. Trey Talley does an excellent job focusing on both. This is a book that needs to be read, not only by teenagers but adults as well."
Rob Zinn, Ph.D., Senior Pastor, Immanuel
Highland, California

"As a high school principal, I tell my students and teachers, 'Everyday you open your eyes you have two choices: roll out or roll over.' *Teenage Construction Zone* gives purpose to rolling out."
- David Ketcher, High School Principal

TEENAGE CONSTRUCTION ZONE PLUS COMPANION BIBLE STUDY

TREY TALLEY

ISBN 13: 978-0-9820141-2-7
ISBN 10: 0-9820141-2-0

Published in 2009 in the United States by
Adsum Press, a division of
Woolstrum Publishing House LLC.

www.adsumpress.com

Printed in the United States of America
on acid-free paper.

16 15 14 13 12 11 10 09 08 07 06 05 04 03 02 01

This book is dedicated to my wonderful daughters,
Allie and Tapanga.
If they are the only ones who ever read this book,
then all of the time and energy spent writing it was
worth it.

Acknowledgements

I thank my best friend in life first, my wife Felisha. She helps me in more ways than she knows. Her stability and enduring love enables me to be free to write and travel as I do.

I thank my daughters for their fun-loving attitudes, the joy they bring, and their ability to keep me laughing. Their smiles motivate me to be the best father I can be.

I thank my parents for providing a stable, loving environment for me to grow up in. Their influence in my life cannot be overstated.

I would also like to thank the ministry of Team Impact for being instrumental in my development as a person.

Teenage Construction Zone

Table of Contents

Table of Contents

Foreword

As a leader and co-founder of Team Impact, I have had the privilege of working alongside Trey Talley for the last twelve years. Trey and I have literally traversed the globe speaking to students of all ages.

Trey is truly a man of integrity. His massive physical stature and numerous body building titles have given him the opportunity to speak in front of millions of students. However, as Trey begins to challenge students with a message of moral purity and positive choices, the students begin to see that real power comes not from lifting weights, but instead from solid moral character. Whether he is speaking to ten people at a local YMCA or thirty thousand people in a soccer stadium in Brazil, his message is the same. Having the tenacity to make good decisions in a world that says there are no moral absolutes is a message that transcends all cultural, racial and economic barriers.

Trey's challenge resonates with so many young people because they recognize that this is a man who truly embodies the principles he espouses. Young people readily identify those that are duplicitous. I have observed some who attempt to urge Trey to "soften" his message so that it will sound more politically correct. But fortunately, Trey's incredible character and the unchanging standard upon which his message is based could not be shaken.

In his book *Teenage Construction Zone*, Trey is able to give students truth that stands in stark contrast to the moral relativism that so many force upon this generation. His message is delivered in such a way that students will be encouraged, challenged, and ultimately changed. His knowledge was not gleaned from a text book. Trey's advice is based upon his direct interaction and dialogue with hundreds of thousands of administrators, teachers and students. Trey's challenge needs to be heard by every student of this generation so that they can construct their life on principles that will build their future to be one of success.

- Jeff Neal, leader of Team Impact
Former NFL's Strongest Man

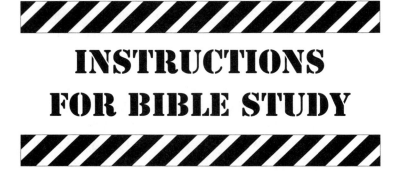

INSTRUCTIONS FOR BIBLE STUDY

Teenage Construction Zone is written as a tool for public schools as well as church groups. If you are using the book in a Christian environment and would like to further substantiate the key points in the book, this is for you.

This Bible study is designed as a companion to Teenage Construction Zone: Building a Strong Foundation for a Great Life.

If you are doing this Bible study on your own, you should:

1. Commit to starting and finishing the book.
2. Read one chapter at a time.
3. Complete the questions for each chapter after you have read the chapter.

Instructions for leaders of small groups, youth groups, and Sunday Schools:

1. This material was designed as a twelve week course.
2. The Bible study is designed to be completed in a group setting the following week, not as home work.
3. Students should be assigned one chapter a week but should wait to answer the questions in class.
4. The leader should read the chapter to be taught before class and circle key paragraphs that could be used to strengthen the points of the book. During class refer back to the book and have students read key sentences or paragraphs. Encourage students to mark or circle points in the book that they find particularly interesting.

5. The leader should also read the questions to be answered before class, so that they will have a well rounded understanding of the chapter, the scriptures, and the questions to be used.

6. During class, alternate between reading selections from the book, the verses, and the questions.

7. At the end of each chapter an "Exercise" has been assigned to help apply the principle to their life. Depending on how much time you have, you can use several methods to do this:

   - Allow ten minutes or more of silence at the beginning of class for the students to read the scriptures and answer the questions on their own, then lead the group by reading key points from the book, scriptures and questions. Open it up for discussion as you see fit.

   - Allow several five minute periods of silence to complete one, two, or three questions. Then stop them and go over the reading selections from the book, scriptures and question. Open it up for discussion as you see fit.

   - Read a selection from the book, the scripture and the questions out loud. Then allow students to discuss and answer out loud. Keep control, and be ready to direct the conversations down the right track.

“I made it. People laughed and said it couldn't be done. But I'm getting married next week, and I am still a virgin.”

- Taylor, 24 (Austin, TX)

“My Parents fight all the time. I wish there was something I could do to make them stop. If I get married, *I hope I don't end up like them.*”

- Sam, 13 (Colorado Springs, CO)

“I am pregnant. It wasn't supposed to be like this. What do I do now?”

- Sarah, 16 (Seattle, WA)

“What a dream come true! I get paid to do what I love to do. It took a lot of work through school, but I did it.”

- Jordan, 22 (Los Angeles, CA)

“Why do they want me to drink so bad? I don't want to, but **I don't want to lose my friends either.**”

- Bailey, 14 (Little Rock, AR)

“Wow, my fourth time to get dumped this year. What's going on? Do I need to do something different?”

- Trace, 17 (Tampa, FL)

“'*Just take one hit*' is what he said. Now, look at me. I can't even stop for one day. What am I supposed to do? I feel so trapped.”

- Wes, 18 (Madison, WI)

TEENAGE CONSTRUCTION ZONE

No matter what anyone tells you, being a teenager is not easy. Some of the most important and challenging decisions of your life are being made right now. Your teenage years can be an exciting but stressful time.

You are at a point in your life where everyone expects you to perform. Your parents expect you to make good grades in school. Coaches expect you to win. Band directors expect you to play well. Your friends expect you to act a certain way, and of course, you have expectations for yourself.

So many expectations! No wonder being a teenager isn't easy. How do you get it right? You have more freedom to think for yourself and more opportunities to act on your own than ever before. But what are you going to do with this new freedom? What type of decisions are you going to make? What do you stand for? What do you define as right and wrong?

You are making thousands of decisions each day, and those choices are shaping your future. This is a critical time in your life. How you choose to live your life now, will impact everything that is to come. Trust me on that.

I have seen so many things I would like to change. I have seen young people in prison for twenty years, pregnant, injured, heartbroken, and empty inside, having to live life in regret because of what they did as a teenager.

But I have also seen the consequences of a young life well lived: dreams achieved, college graduates, successful careers, healthy marriages, great friendships. I have seen people who are stable, full of joy, and satisfied with life.

What about you? If you could improve your life, would you? If you could improve the lives of those around you, would you? Of course you would, and the good news is that you can! You don't have to settle for less. You don't have to follow in the tracks of bad examples around you. You can pave your own road. How? By making the right choices.

I have created this book to offer you tools and guidance for the choices that you will make in this critical time. I want to help you build a life with no regrets. I want to help you deal with your problems, dilemmas, and everyday choices. I want you to have the greatest life you possibly can. My hope is that by taking the time to read and apply this book, you'll be well on your way to achieve just that.

THE FOUNDATION OF YOUR LIFE

CHAPTER 1

Driving through Dallas, Texas, I came across a huge construction site. Large projects like this are always amazing to me, so I stopped to get a better look. There were hundreds of people and massive machines working on the foundation of what was soon to be one of the top hotels in the Dallas area. It was obvious, even to the untrained eye, that an enormous amount of detail was going into the foundation of this building to insure proper stability, durability, and strength.

The entire building's integrity would be forever dependent on this foundation. Imagine the pressure these guys must have felt. Millions of dollars, as well as the safety of thousands of people, were riding on the construction team to build this foundation correctly.

Of course, engineers fully understand the importance of a strong foundation. They frequently inspect it to make sure that it is being constructed to their specifications. They know that the integrity of the foundation is absolutely essential to the rest of the construction process. There is no room for shortcuts or mistakes. Everything needs to be perfect.

Like that hotel in Dallas, you are in the most important stage of your life. Whether you realize it or not, you are constructing the foundation that the rest of your life will be placed upon. While the foundation of a hotel is made of thousands of pieces of concrete, metal, brick, mortar, and other building materials, your life's foundation is being constructed with the choices that you are making. That is why it is critical to understand the importance of a single choice. Every choice you make is a building block for your life.

> *Every choice you make is a building block for your life.*

If you think about these choices and choose wisely, then you will construct a strong stable foundation on which to live your life. If you make the wrong choices, you will construct a foundation that is very weak and unstable. Your future will be the result of the choices that you are making now. No pressure, right?

In the construction of a building's foundation, strength is definitely the key to success. With today's technology, it's easy for engineers to analyze the strength of a foundation and predict its reliability with great certainty. With humans, however, it can be a little more difficult. Or so we think.

While it's not as easy as plugging in a machine and waiting for the results, we can analyze our foundations and even predict their reliability with some certainty. How? By observing the quality of our daily choices.

With every choice that you have made, with every choice that you are making now, and with every choice that you will make, you are adding one more brick to your foundation. What you choose to do at school, at home, on a date, or look at on the internet are all decisions that are shaping your life's foundation. If you are daily making strong decisions in these areas, then your foundation will be unshakable.

The choices are being made, the bricks are being laid. The question is, are you building a foundation that will be strong enough to support the quality life that you desire?

Are you building a foundation that will be strong enough?

Foundational Regrets

As a motivational speaker, I speak to people in all types of environments – churches, schools, juvenile detention centers, community gatherings, etc. On one such occasion, I was speaking at a prison to a large group of inmates. After the general presentation, one of the inmates asked to speak with me privately. I had a little extra time, and he had nothing but time. So I made my way deep into the cell blocks of this high security prison with a guard.

I've seen prison shows on TV. But walking into a prison,

feeling the weight of the windowless building press down on you, the never ending sight of concrete and metal doors, witnessing it personally – it was altogether different.

We passed through stringent security and about ten huge locked doors before the guard finally said that we had arrived at the inmate's cell. As we entered, I was immediately struck with a strong sense of claustrophobia. The room was eight feet wide by nine feet long, not much bigger than a pool table. The walls, ceiling, and floor were all bare concrete.

The cold metal door shut behind us. Only a tiny window provided any view of the outside hallway. On one side of the cell, a small twin size mattress fit snuggly into a stainless steel shelf. In the opposite corner of the cell was another solitary stainless steel appliance, combining a toilet and sink into one.

There was nothing else. He had absolutely nothing to do and nothing to see. I could tell that he was glad just to talk with someone on the outside.

After only a few minutes of small talk, the guard told me it was already time to go. Before I left, I couldn't help but wonder about what got him into prison, so I politely asked him,

"Jake, if you don't mind me asking, where did things go wrong?"

I thought he would need a while to think about my question and gather his thoughts, but he didn't. He had already been in prison for seven years, and had about thirteen more years left. He had nothing to do each day except analyze his past and see what lead him here, so without hesitating, he answered,

"It was my eighth grade year. If it wasn't for my eighth grade year, I wouldn't be here today."

I was very surprised by his answer, so I asked him,

"What could you have possibly done in the eighth grade to land you in prison?"

In the eighth grade, Jake's best friend had gotten him to take his first drink of beer. The next day, they went back to school and bragged about what they had done. He told me how he liked that sense of rebellion and the extra attention that he received from others. As a result, he began to drink on a regular basis. The problem got much worse as he went through high school. He would get so drunk, he wouldn't even remember what happened at the party the night before. Entire pieces of his life were just missing.

One day, he woke up to find himself in jail. Because of the drunken stupor he had been in, he had no recollection of the previous night's tragic events. He thought he had been arrested for being drunk in public. He didn't even realize that he had committed a horrible crime that would change his life forever. The night before, he had left a party, gotten into his car, and ended the lives of two people in a head-on collision. Two innocent lives tragically came to an end that night.

As Jake reflected on that awful morning, tears began to roll down his prison hardened face. There was no hiding his emotions. He knew he had made a huge mistake, and now he had to pay the price.

"Not a day goes by that I don't wish I could go back and change things," he said.

My time was up. The guard and I exited the room. The guard shut and locked the huge metal door, and we made the journey back to the front of the prison. As I walked past the endless row of metal doors, behind each of which was a prisoner, I couldn't help but wonder, how many, if not all, were there because of a choice they made in their youth?

The Choice is Yours

The power of a bad foundational choice was painfully obvious with Jake. He knew the exact moment where things went wrong. He understood that had it not been for his decision to take his first drink, there wouldn't have been a second, third, fourth and so on. He understood that if it hadn't been for that decision in the eighth grade, two people would still be alive, and he would not be locked up like an animal in a little cage with twenty years of his life gone.

> The average person makes 4,000 choices a day!

However, the choice had been made, the brick had been laid, and now the price had to be paid. Jake understands now the powerful effect of foundational choices, but his understanding came at an extremely high price.

Every day, every moment, you are confronted with a new challenge, a new choice. The average person makes around

4,000 choices a day! In other words, every day of your life, four thousand bricks are being added to your foundation. Will you make the right choice – or the wrong choice?

The choices you have made in the past define who you are today. Who you will be and where you will be in twenty years will depend on the decisions that you are making right now. You will be who you make yourself to be.

> *The choices you have made in the past define who you are today.*

If you consistently place the right bricks on your foundation in all areas of your life, then you will build a foundation that has the strength to support an incredible future. Remember, you are the engineer and the architect of your future! What you build is up to you!

THE FOUNDATION OF YOUR LIFE
WEEK 1

"[You are] built on the foundation of the apostles and prophets, with Christ Jesus himself as the chief cornerstone. In him the whole building is joined together and rises to become a holy temple in the Lord. And in him you too are being built together to become a dwelling in which God lives by his Spirit." (Ephesians 2:20-22)

1. We as Christians should be even more cautious while we build, because according to this Scripture, what are we building?

____

____

2. Read the verse again. Believers are joined together in the work of Christ. This project takes all types of people to complete the job. Are you doing your share? Could you do more? What are some things you could do to help others grow stronger in Christ?

____

____

Group Discussion

"Show me your ways, O Lord, teach me your paths; guide me in your truth and teach me, for you are God my Savior, and my hope is in you all day long." (Psalm 25:4-5)

Really think for a moment about what you are using as your blue print to live life. Where did you learn to act the way that you do? Why do you act the way you do? Discuss possible blueprints that you or others are using to guide you through life.

3. As we build, what should we use as our supreme blueprint for life?

Have you ever tried to put something together without reading the directions? It usually doesn't work. Some people try to build their lives without ever reading the instructions. Are you reading the Bible as you build or are you expecting to have a great life without reading the Instruction Book?

4. What if your prayer each day included Psalm 25:4-5? Would you be more likely to rely on God? God wants to be your teacher and guide in life. Will you let him?

"Do not be deceived: God cannot be mocked. A man reaps what he sows. The one who sows to please his sinful nature, from that nature will reap destruction; the one who sows to please the Spirit, from the Spirit will reap eternal life." (Galatians 6:7-8)

"The evil deeds of a wicked man ensnare him; the cords of his sin hold him fast. He will die for

lack of discipline, led astray by his own great folly."
(Proverbs 5:22-23)

5. How do these verses relate to Chapter 1's idea of "building your life."

____

____

6. Can you give an example of reaping and sowing in your own life? Give an example of when your actions had an obvious consequence.

____

____

____

____

"Therefore everyone who hears these words of mine and puts them into practice is like a wise man who built his house on the rock. The rain came down, the streams rose, and the winds blew and beat against that house; yet it did not fall, because it had its foundation on the rock. But everyone who hears these words of mine and does not put them into practice is like a foolish man who built his house on sand."
(Mathew 7:24-26)

7. How do we make sure that our lives are built on rock and not sand?

____

____

Group Discussion

Can bad things happen to Christians? Then what is the benefit of being a Christian if we can get hit with the same storms?

____

____

"…make the most of every opportunity." (Colossians 4:5b)

"And we pray this in order that you may live a life worthy of the Lord and may please him in every way: bearing fruit in every good work, growing in the knowledge of God…" (Colossians 1:10)

8. Are you "making the most of every opportunity"? Are you living a life that will "please him in every way"?

____

9. According to Jake, how many bad choices did it take to destroy his foundation? ____________

Exercise: List three things about your foundation that could use a little strengthening.

1. ______________________________________

____

2. ______________________________________

____

3. ______________________________________

____

YOUR FUTURE IS IN YOUR HANDS

CHAPTER 2

Every young person has an idea, dream, or goal, which is good because focusing on the future is a very important attribute of highly successful people. However, successful people don't just set goals for their lives; they take the steps needed to attain them.

Did you catch what I just said? Successful people take the steps needed to attain their goals. The problem most people have is not with creating a goal or dream for their lives, but with the planning required to get them there. They have dreams, but they don't take the steps needed to reach them.

When I was in middle school, I told my friends that I would be a millionaire by the time I was 20. Sounded good, but I had no plan. When I was in high school getting paid five bucks an hour to load farm trucks with bags of animal feed, I realized I probably wasn't going to make it. My "millionaire by 20" dream was obviously never going to be more than just a dream. At the rate of five dollars an hour, it would have taken me over 150 years to become a millionaire.

It's definitely easier to set a goal than to attain that goal. You can set a goal in a matter of moments but reaching it could take weeks, months, years or even a lifetime. Setting a goal is one decision, but accomplishing a goal usually involves thousands of decisions. Having a goal without commitment, consistency, and discipline is just a fantasy!

Having a goal without commitment, consistency, and discipline is just a fantasy!

Big Dream for a Little Guy!

When I was nine years old, I decided that I wanted to become a bodybuilder. Now, this was quite a lofty goal, because I was the skinniest little twig in my class. I had no muscle, and I was the furthest thing possible from looking like a bodybuilder. In fact, I was on the receiving end of quite a number of skinny jokes.

For instance, "Trey, you're so skinny you could hula hoop with a Fruit Loop" or "Man, you are so skinny you could hang-glide from a Dorito."

Becoming a bodybuilder was a pretty farfetched idea for a skinny little kid from the country. I grew up in small country town in Arkansas. I didn't know any bodybuilders. In fact, I don't think I had ever even seen a bodybuilder. There wasn't even a gym to workout in within an hour's drive.

I don't know exactly what led me to become a body-builder, but I did see a program on TV years ago on an issue called the "Barbie Doll Syndrome." The sociologist said that as young girls grow up playing with Barbie dolls, sometimes something happens to a very small percentage of them and they want to look just like Barbie.

I didn't play with Barbie dolls in my little town out in the woods of Arkansas. I didn't have a Ken doll either. No, I had something else. Something big, green and covered in muscles. An action figure. The action figure. That's right. The Incredible Hulk. The strongest man of all time!

I used to love watching the TV series. I found out that the actor who played the Hulk on the TV series was a bodybuilder, so maybe that's where my dream started. Or maybe those jokes in school really went to heart. I doubt that I really had "Barbie Doll Syndrome," or "Incredible Hulk Syndrome," but the dream was there.

I went to my dad and asked him to show me some exercises that would help me get bigger. He showed me how to do push-ups and sit-ups. I'll be honest; at first I could barely do any. Even five push-ups was a struggle, but I didn't give up. I began to do these exercises almost every single day.

As the years went by, my parents saw my commitment and got me a little weight lifting set. I couldn't believe my eyes. I cleared out an old shed behind our house that was used to store junk and turned it into my "gym".

Now, don't let the word gym fool you. The shed was tiny. It was freezing in the winter and scorching hot in the summer. When it rained, the floor of my little gym would flood with about three inches of water, but I didn't let that stop me. I would just put on rain boots and go work out. It took me many years of consistently working out to get to where anyone could even tell that I was lifting weights. However, I persevered, and slowly but surely, I began to get bigger.

> ***Set a goal and take the steps to make it come true.***

When I was seventeen, I went to the University of Arkansas to attend college. It was there that I actually got to enter my first real gym. I was thrilled. Now I had a facility with top of the line equipment to help me actually make this dream come true.

The gym seemed bigger than my whole town. Plus, it had air conditioning and heating, and I didn't even have to wear rain boots to work out! I pursued my dream even more at this point. I worked out up to three hours a day and increased my knowledge by reading books on bodybuilding.

Two years later, I won the Arkansas State Teenage Bodybuilding Competition. The culmination of 10 years of working out, thousands of hours exercising, and a ton of commitment all came together and made it possible for me to achieve my goal that year.

I set a goal that was considered unreachable by many, and I took the steps to make it come true. I didn't accomplish that goal with just one decision to become a bodybuilder. I had to work out approximately 2,000 times over the course of 10 years to make that dream come true.

I share that story with you not to tell you to start doing pushups and sit-ups or to join a gym. Everyone is different and along with that everyone has desires, ambitions, and goals that are unique to them. I shared my story just to let you know that if a guy like me can make his goals come true, then you certainly can too.

Goal Challenge

If you truly want to have a great life, then start taking small practical steps in the right direction to turn your dreams into realities. Great dreams require great preparation. As the old saying goes "Rome was not built in a day" and neither are your dreams. Success usually doesn't happen by accident.

> *Great dreams require great preparation.*

If you want to achieve something, it's important to determine what that "something" is. How can you achieve your goals if you never set them? What does your ideal future look like?

Seriously, think about it for a second. Stop reading, close your eyes, and think about how you would like your life to be in ten years. Are you a movie star living in Hollywood? Are you living in a mansion with butlers and maids at your command? Are you rolling in piles of money on the floor? Are you driving the latest $100,000 Mercedes Benz?

These might be the first dreams that come to your mind, but I encourage you to think deeper. The examples above are all pretty materialistic. Try to think about what really matters.

How about a job that you enjoy waking up to everyday? What's your passion and what do you want to do with it? Do you play sports? Maybe you should be a coach and teach others the love of the game. Are you good at math? Maybe you can help build and launch the next NASA space flight. Or maybe you're the person who likes to cook, who will one day be a world famous chef. Do you like to write? To paint? To decorate? To fix cars? To sing? To play an instrument?

How about a spouse who loves everything about you and is committed to loving you every day of your life? Do you want to get married? At what age and to what kind of person? Will you have kids eventually, or not? Where would you like to live?

And you? What do you want to be like years from now? Will you be a respected leader? Will people look up to you in the community? Will you be a voice of reason to those around you? Will you be an amazing parent or spouse that others look to for support?

Be specific! If you don't think about your own future, then who will?

Goal Exercise

Now, take a moment to get those thoughts in ink. Find a blank piece of paper and a pen. Now, list at least ten things: accomplishments, successes, or characteristics that you would like to have or accomplish within the next ten years. Leave spaces in between them. If you have more than ten, great!

If you want to build something great, it's going to take preparation, planning, and thought.

As you look over your list, ask yourself if you are doing what it takes to get you there. We know that setting goals is great, but that's the easy part! Underneath each goal, I want you to list two actions that are going to get you closer to achieving it.

I know this may take a moment of deep thought, but I guarantee you it's worth it. By taking a moment to really envision your future, you are taking your first steps towards making it come true.

If you put a specific career, then what is going to get you closer? Better grades? Attending college?

If you wrote down that you want to be respected, then maybe you should write to treat others with more respect. By giving respect, you will begin to receive it.

No engineer just starts piling bricks up, randomly expecting an architectural masterpiece to somehow form. It takes a lot of preparation, planning, and thought. So it is with your life! If you want to build something great, it's going to take preparation, planning, and thought as well. In construction, they use a blueprint, a detailed drawing of how to turn bricks, metal, and mortar into a wonderful building.

I want to encourage you to put some thought into the goal exercise that was just covered. Put that piece of paper somewhere you can see it. Check it often. Use it as part of your blueprint to make sure that you are building the life you desire.

Inspecting Your Foundation

Now that you have thought about your future, do you believe that your foundation, the way it is currently being built, is going to support your dreams and goals? If the answer is no, then take a moment to identify the weak spots in your foundation. On the back of your sheet of paper, write down what the problem is and how you plan on fixing it.

> *If your foundation has bad bricks, stop everything, evaluate the problem, and fix it before you go any further.*

If engineers realized that the foundation of a major building was not being constructed properly, they would stop all construction, evaluate the problem, and fix it before they went any further. They know that if they continued to build a weak foundation, the entire building would be jeopardized. It's the same with people. If you realize that your foundation has some bad bricks, then stop everything, evaluate the problem, and fix it before you go any further. You are the architect and the engineer. You are in control. Plan it out. Make it happen!

YOUR FUTURE IS IN YOUR HANDS
WEEK 2

"Unless the Lord builds the house, its builders labor
in vain." (Psalm 127:1a)

1. Building in vain means living for earthly pleasure instead of seeking God. Can you think of people who build in vain? Do you personally build in vain sometimes?

Give two examples:

1. ____

____

2. ____

____

"Since, then you have been raised with Christ,
set your hearts on things above, where Christ
is seated at the right hand of God. Set your
minds on things above, not on earthly things."
(Colossians 3:1-2)

2. As we think about what we want our lives to be like, we should not just consider what we want out of life, but what God wants out of our life. We do this by setting our _________ and our _______ on things above. This takes continual effort to do. In this life it is quite easy to get absorbed into earthly living, and not on things above.

How often do you look to God for advice? Are your heart and mind set on what God wants with your life or just what you want?

"… I urge you to live a life worthy of the calling you have received." (Ephesians 4:1)

3. Is it enough to live our lives in order to please ourselves, our friends, or parents? Why?

___

___

Group Discussion

"For we brought nothing into the world, and we can take nothing out of it." (1 Timothy 6:7)

We are on earth for a matter of years. We will be in eternity forever. Yet many Christians build for success only in this life. Discuss why that happens to so many.

"Keep your lives free from the love of money and be content with what you have, because God has said, 'Never will I leave you; never will I forsake you.'" (Hebrews 13:5)

"People who want to get rich fall into temptation and a trap and into many foolish and harmful desires that plunge men into ruin and destruction. For the love of money is a root of all kinds of evil. Some people, eager for money, have wandered from the faith and pierced themselves with many griefs." (1 Timothy 6:9-10)

4. Is wanting to make money wrong? Remember this verse doesn't say that "money is a root of all kinds of evil." Instead it says, "the ______ of money is a root of all kinds of evil." How can obtaining riches quickly turn into sin?

____

____

"Do not store up for yourselves treasures on earth, where moth and rust destroy, and where thieves break in and steal. But store up for yourselves treasures in heaven where moth and rust do not destroy, and where thieves do not break in and steal. For where your treasure is, there your heart will be also." (Mathew 6:19-21)

5. Having goals and dreams is fine, as long as they don't become your all consuming drive. It is important to remember that one day you will be gone, and everything you have worked hard for will be left here. With that in mind, what are your goals for this life?

Exercise

Before continuing, complete the Goal Exercise portion from Chapter 2 on the space provided on the next page.

Goal Exercise

YOU ARE SHAPING YOUR LIFE!

CHAPTER 3

Many young people will one day attain the life they have always desired because they have consistently, over time, placed the right bricks on their foundation. However, it saddens me that many will not find such pleasure. One day, those people will realize that the foundation that they have been building to reach their dreams simply will not be strong enough.

How do you avoid this happening to you? You have already begun. Just taking the time to read this book reveals that you're already putting more thought into your future than most people ever do. But it takes more than just reading a book to truly change your life. It takes a realization. You must learn to constantly live your life with the realization that the choices you are making today are determining the quality of your future.

I know that factors exist in your environment that are

> Take control of where your life is heading.

outside of your control, but you are the one building your life's foundation. Take control of where your life is heading.

Some people have no idea of where they are going or how to get there. They usually just follow whatever is the path of least resistance. It's time to get out of the passenger seat, and learn to steer! Take your life where it needs to be going. Make every choice with purpose. Not because it's what's easiest, but because you want the best for yourself.

But You Don't Know My Situation!

When some people find that their lives did not turn out the way they wanted them to, they look back and blame other people, their surroundings, or their circumstances. But from what I have seen, we are who we are because we made ourselves this way. As Chuck Swindoll, the inspirational author, once said, "Life is 10% what happens to you, and 90% of what you do with it."[1]

You may not be in control of everything that happens to you, but you are in control of how you handle it. Everyone has problems; it's how you deal with the problems that makes the difference. Successful people are those

> Everyone has problems; it's how you deal with the problems that makes the difference.

that handle the situation, and don't let the situation handle them.

It's My Parents Fault

One day, I was speaking to a school assembly in Wichita, Kansas on the effects of drugs and alcohol. After the assembly, a fourteen year old young lady named Samantha came over to talk with me. Samantha told me that her mom and dad were both alcoholics, and that this had made her become an alcoholic as well. Although only in the seventh grade, she had already been through Alcoholics Anonymous.

As I heard her story, my heart went out to her. It is so sad to see a young person going through life with parents that are such bad examples. However, I have lived long enough to know that just because a person's parents are alcoholics, doesn't mean that they are required to become one as well. It might be easier for that person to find an excuse to become an alcoholic like their parents, but the bottom line is that each person is responsible for their own choices.

I have a close friend named Berry that I have worked with for thirteen years. He grew up with an alcoholic father that kept a full service bar in their house. Each day, he watched his father drink away his health and his abilities to lead a normal life. Despite the pressure from his father to take a drink, he never took a single one. He is 40 years old today and still has never had a drink of any kind of alcohol.

Samantha and Berry are two people with very similar

home lives who took totally opposite paths. The first used her parents' alcohol abuse as an excuse to begin doing the same things they were doing. The other saw what the alcohol did to his father and chose never to allow it into his body. Both saw the chaos that alcohol brought into their homes, yet each had to decide for themselves what they were going to do with their experience.

I know that many people don't have the opportunity to grow up in a perfect home. In fact, many of you are probably growing up in awful home situations. You may face challenges that some of your friends do not. But you still have the ability to create a great life for yourself.

> *Even if you are growing up in an awful home situation, you still have the ability to create a great life for yourself.*

Even though you have been through or are going through various types of turmoil at home, never use it as an excuse to make the same mistakes that you have seen others close to you make. By making the right choices, by laying different bricks on your foundation, you don't have to be like any of the negative role models that you have seen.

Often times alcoholics beget alcoholics, drug addicts beget drug addicts, abusers beget abusers, etc. The cycle continues generation after generation. But you can be the one to break the cycle. You have seen what those types of choices produce, and the type of lives they create. Don't think you can put the same bricks on your foundation and expect a different result! Life has enough difficulties without creating additional struggles.

Excuses, Excuses!

Always look for the way to succeed, not the excuse for failure! Excuses are readily available, and are easily found, especially in today's society where no one seems to take responsibility for their own actions.

People who smoke cigarettes get cancer and blame the company that manufactured them. Even though they smoked two packs a day for thirty years, they want to blame someone else. People become alcoholics and blame it on a disease, not their own lack of self-control. Addicts blame their addiction on their friends or how hard their life is. Women starve themselves and blame it on fashion models.

I was watching the news the other day and was amazed at the extreme people will go to in order not to take the blame. A married man sued a flower company after he paid them to send flowers to his girlfriend. Now remember, he was married to someone else. He was upset because he said the flower company sent a receipt of the delivery to his house. His wife saw the receipt and realized what was happening. Needless to say, she filed for divorce.

The man ended up suing the flower company for exposing his affair to his wife. Absolutely ridiculous! The flower company had nothing to do with his immoral behavior, but people always want to blame something or someone else for their own mistakes.

It seems like blaming others for our own mistakes is one of the first things we learn to do as humans. My youngest daughter started this at age two. She would blame our dogs for just about everything. Once, we were travelling from Texas and staying in a hotel in Orlando, Florida. At the hotel, my daughter had made a mess, so I asked her "Who did that?"

Without hesitation, she answered, "The dogs did it." Unfortunately for her, we had left the dogs fifteen hours away back in Texas.

When you take responsibility for your own actions, you will get to the root of the problem.

It is so much easier for people to look elsewhere for the blame. It is much harder to take a deep look within ourselves first. If you realize that you have messed up, then fess up, take responsibility, and get back on track. When you take responsibility for your own actions, you will get to the root of the problem. When you don't, the blame will be put on other people or other situations that you have no control over.

Do you want your parents to dress you every morning? Of course not! Your freedom to choose what you wear is something that you couldn't dream of giving up to someone else. Likewise, the ability to decide what you do with your life is a priceless gift. By blaming others, you lose control of the ability to fix the problems in your life.

Don't give away your freedom to decide who you want to be. Don't let someone else decide your life for you. Remember, it's easier to change yourself than to change everything and everyone around you. Take ownership of your life. Don't shift responsibility. Instead, realize that ultimately, you are responsible for you!

Abuse

While I know what most teenagers face, I do not pretend to know your exact struggles. Yes, I am encouraging you to take responsibility for your own foundation by not blaming others for your problems.

But, part of taking responsibility for your foundation may mean getting help. If you are being abused, especially physically or sexually, then you need to get help.

If you are being abused, you need to get help!

If that is the case, I want you to know that abuse is absolutely wrong in every situation. You did not do anything to deserve being abused. *Get help immediately!* Let someone outside of the situation know about the abuse today. Talk to a counselor, teacher, principle, police officer, pastor, youth leader, a friend, your friend's parents, or anyone else you know that can help you.

It Is Never Time to Give Up!

Try to remember that it's not how you start the race that counts, but how you finish it. Simply put, you might have had a rough start because of your choices or surroundings. You might be struggling in the race of life, but it is never too late for a comeback!

I'm sure you could find a perfectly good reason to give up on your dreams or to just give in to the negative pressures that might be around you. But don't do it. There is still time to create a successful life. Your foundation is still being constructed. If you've had a bad past, don't beat yourself up about it. And definitely don't dwell on it! That accomplishes nothing. Instead, learn from it and move on. You can't go back and make a new beginning, but you can start today to make a new ending!

YOU ARE SHAPING YOUR LIFE!
WEEK 3

Group Review

Briefly look over last week's lesson. What changes did the discussion bring in your life, your actions, your thoughts, or your relationship with God?

> "If any man builds on this foundation using gold, silver, costly stones, wood, hay or straw, his work will be shown for what it is, because the Day will bring it to light. It will be revealed with fire, and the fire will test the quality of each man's work. If what he has built survives, he will receive his reward. If it is burned up, he will suffer loss; he himself will be saved, but only as one escaping through the flames."
> (1 Corinthians 3:12-15)

1. Some Christians build their lives with things that will not matter in eternity. These things will be "burned up." What are some things in your life that are not going to last in eternity?

____

____

2. What are some things in your life that will last in eternity?

____

3. When people run out from a house fire, do they get to bring much with them? Why does Paul use this analogy to compare some Christians who are entering Heaven?

"Therefore, my dear brothers, stand firm. Let nothing move you. Always give yourselves fully to the work of the Lord, because you know that your labor in the Lord is not in vain." (1 Corinthians 15:58)

4. Everyone goes through tough times. What are some practical things that you can do in order to help you stand firm?

"Don't let anyone look down on you because you are young, but set an example for the believers in speech, in life, in love, in faith and in purity." (1Timothy 4:12)

Group Discussion

Do you think some young Christians use their youthfulness to excuse sin in their lives? Do you ever do the same?

5. How can you set an example for others in your:

Speech?

Life?

____

Love?

____

Faith?

____

Purity?

____

"Be very careful, then, how you live—not as unwise but as wise, making the most of every opportunity, because the days are evil. Therefore do not be foolish, but understand what the Lord's will is." (Ephesians 5:15-17)

6. We are commanded to be wise builders, by understanding what the _______________ is. We can find his will through his word, through prayer, and through fellow believers.

"A man reaps what he sows. The one who sows to please his sinful nature, from that nature, will reap destruction; the one who sows to please the Spirit, from the Spirit will reap eternal life. Let us not become weary in doing good, for at the proper time we will reap a harvest if we do not give up." (Galatians 6:7b-10)

7. No matter how tiresome doing good may seem, it is worth it. If you don't give up you will reap a great ____________. For a farmer, a good harvest was the reward of a lot of labor like planting, weeding, fertilizing, and watering. If they did all of those things, then they

could expect a great harvest. As you continue to do good works in all areas of your life, you can expect a harvest of good things as well.

> "At the end of your life you will groan, when your flesh and body are spent. You will say, 'How I hated discipline! How my heart spurned correction! I would not obey my teachers or listen to my instructors. I have come to the brink of utter ruin in the midst of the whole assembly.'" (Proverbs 5:11-14)

8. This is the opposite of a good harvest. Do you ever hate discipline or not obey people in authority like your parents, church leaders, teachers, or police? If so, change immediately, or reap the harvest.

Exercise

Look back over your Goal Exercise Worksheet. In light of what you have learned, do you think that your goals would line up with God's plan for your life? If not, spend a moment writing in the changes.

FRIENDS: THE CONSTRUCTION CREW

CHAPTER 4

Buildings like that hotel in Dallas must go through many stages of construction before they can be pronounced complete. After the architect draws the blueprints and the engineers approve them, they are sent to a general contractor. This person oversees the construction of the building.

He or she hires different crews of laborers that are specialized in their specific area of construction. For example, the first crew lays the foundation. The next crew raises the frame of the building. Other crews will do the plumbing, electrical work, and interior walls.

Each stage of the building process has to happen in the right order. You can't put up a frame until you have the foundation in place. Nor can you put up interior walls or windows without a frame to hold them there. Each crew of workers builds upon the work that was done by the last crew.

Therefore, the earlier on in the building process, the more critical that step will be.

Right now, your life is under construction, just like that building. Does anyone build a building by themselves? Of course not! There are always whole crews of laborers. The laborers are the ones who actually make the building happen.

You are the general contractor of your life. You may decide who is going to influence the construction of your building, but the people who influence you, your friends, are the laborers.

Since your decisions during this time of your life are so important, it is also just as important to choose the right people to be on your construction crew. They will drastically affect the quality of what you build by the influence that they have. Friends will either help you build your foundation for a lifetime of success or a lifetime of heartache.

Friends will either help you build your foundation for a lifetime of success or a lifetime of heartache.

Just how much power friends have during these formative years depends on how much power you allow them to have. Many young people let their friends have too much control over the construction of their life's foundation. Did you know that the number one reason that a person takes their first drink of alcohol is because of a friend? The same is true for drugs and nearly every other high risk activity.

At this point in your life, you probably feel an immense amount of pressure to fit in. That's normal. Everyone wants to have a sense of belonging, especially among their friends. But if you have friends that are constructing bad foundations for their lives, your desire to fit in can make you even more susceptible to making a choice that you know is not right.

This is nothing new. It's an age old problem that has plagued humankind since the beginning of time. Even a famous writing from 2,000 years ago states that "bad company corrupts good character." Or as my Granddad would always say, "One bad apple ruins the whole bunch." If you put a rotten apple in with other good ones, it makes the others start to rot. The same can be said of people.

Think for a moment about the people that you consider your closest friends. What are they like? How do they act and treat people? What types of interests do they have? What are their views about others, themselves, their parents, or the rest of life?

Then think about how your friends have affected some of your choices already. Some of those influences might be insignificant like clothing and hairstyles, but some influences can be very serious and have lasting effects.

What about your friends? Do they care how well your building is built, or do they just care about themselves? Will your friends help you build a strong foundation for life, or will they leave it cracked and broken?

Friend? Acquaintance? Or Enemy?

Sometimes we are a little too loose with the title "friend."

> A true friend is someone who will always back you up in making the right choices in life.

A true friend is not just someone that you hang out with at school. That just makes them someone you spend time with. A true friend is someone who will always back you up in making the right choices in life.

Are your friends doing that for you? Are you doing that for them? A real friend will do everything in their power to help you have a great life now and a great future later. They are not going to encourage you to make decisions that hurt you or sit idly by and allow you to make these destructive choices. Friends don't try to destroy your life. That's what enemies do!

Looking back on my own life, I can see that some of the people I called my friends really didn't fit the definition of friend at all. If I had allowed certain childhood friends to stay close friends, my life would be a whole lot different than it is now. As the years went by, some of the people I used to call close friends had to have that status taken away.

My best friend growing up had a great personality. He was the class clown and super easy to get along with. We had a blast no matter what we were doing. But by the 11th grade, he started hanging out with some guys who were on their way to nowhere. Along with their new friendship, he became more and more like them, which typically meant lots of partying, drinking, and so on. I had a tough decision to make, but I knew that I had to distance myself from him. It wasn't easy, but I knew I had to do it.

By the time I got to the 12th grade, I really only had three people that could be called true friends. That might seem a bit sad at first, but as you go through life, you will find that it's not about how many friends you have. It's about how good of friends you have.

A True Friend is Better than Gold (or a Credit Card)!

Inside cliques or social groups, friends usually have something in common. In other words, people who have similar interests usually like being around each other. Birds of a feather flock together. A group of friends might all share an interest in something constructive like football, music, dancing, or art. Or, their interest may be in something destructive like smoking, drug use, bullying, gossiping, etc.

When you hang around friends with a mutual interest, you are strengthening your attraction to that interest. This can be a good or bad thing depending on what the interest is. Obviously the desire to be a better athlete or dancer is great. But a strong desire to drink or smoke is not so great. Either way, it's important to realize the power that your close friends have on you. Your friendships are either going to strengthen or weaken your life's foundation. It's going to happen, whether you like it or not.

I knew a group of guys in my college dorm who were friends simply because they liked to drink. Anytime they were together, that was all they wanted to talk about. They would talk about when they got drunk last, how crazy they acted the last time they got drunk, or when the next party was. By doing this, it strengthened their resolve to continue drinking. They were encouraging each other to drink even more.

What happens if one of them decides to never drink again? He might find that he didn't have as much in common with them as he thought. Hopefully, he will begin to befriend others who have a similar stand on that issue. But what if he doesn't? What if he stays friends with those same guys that are consumed with drinking, even though he has decided that he is not going to drink anymore? He will feel pressure to fit in with his friends. He won't want to be the odd man out by not drinking. Therefore, the odds are very high that he will eventually drink again.

> The more you hang out with a person, the more you begin to act like that person.

You need to choose your friends wisely because you will become a lot like them. The more you hang out with a person, the more you begin to act like that person. I love the old proverb that says, "As iron sharpens iron, so one man sharpens another." In other words, people influence each other.

Likewise, you are sharpened or dulled by the fellow humans you hang around. Your friends greatly influence your day to day life, the construction of your life's foundation, and your future. Are your friends sharpening your life? Are they making you even better? Remember, if you want to be great, then hang around great people.

A Change of Friends?

Many young people honestly try to change the direction of their lives for the better. However, they end up falling back to those same old paths they were on before because they failed to change friends.

Before long they are looking and acting just like those friends again. They thought they were strong enough to resist, or even strong enough to help their friends up. But somewhere in the process, they got pulled down all over again.

Trying to pull someone up morally is very difficult. It's kind of like trying to pull someone up out of the swimming pool while you are standing on the edge. You have to be very careful because in your effort to help, you are also in a vulnerable position to get pulled in. It would be much easier for someone in a pool to pull you in than for you to pull them out.

Mike was a man in his early thirties that had volunteered to drive me around to various speaking events one week while I was in Alabama. While driving one day, he told me that he had hung around with a bad crowd in high school and ended up with seven felonies when he was 18 years old. Not something you really want to hear about a stranger that's going to be driving you around all week, but I could tell that he wasn't the same guy anymore.

He had spent several hard years in prison for his crimes. When his time was up, he was released back into society to start a new life. Everyone, including him, thought that he had finally learned his lesson. But he went right back to those old friends that he ran with when he was eighteen.

Before long, he was acting just like them all over again. He ended up back in prison with more felonies. Once again, he did his time and got out a couple years later. This time, however, he really did learn his lesson. As I talked with him only months after he had been out of prison for the second time, I asked him, "What's going to make the difference this time?"

His reply was simple, but correct.

"A change of friends!" he said.

In fact, Mike moved away and changed his address and phone number to break ties with those who were bad influences on him. He became very active in a local church, and began to surround himself with people who would truly help him. He had learned his lesson, but that lesson cost him about six years of his life. While it's possible to stand up for what is right by yourself, it sure is easier when you are with others who are doing the same.

Finding the right friends can be very difficult. Realizing that you might need to change friends can be even more difficult. But the payoff is worth it. True friends can strengthen your will to stay the course and have a great life.

Did you know that geese fly 70% further than they could alone because of the teamwork they use while flying in a V formation? The geese in the front of the formation create air currents that make it easier for the geese in the back of the formation to fly. When the goose in the front grows weary, another one takes its place, allowing the one in front to go further down in the lineup where it is easier to fly.

What's also interesting about geese is how loud they are when they are flying in this formation. We'll never know what they are truly saying, but maybe they're encouraging each other. "Keep going, were almost there, don't give up." Or who knows, they could be saying, "Are we there yet? I need to go to the bathroom!"

Like the geese, friends that encourage you are a huge asset. They can help you stay the course by strengthening you when you're weak and by encouraging when you need it most. The right friends with the right mindset are a great blessing in anyone's life.

Join the Crew

Remember that your friends are a vital part of your construction crew but don't forget that you are a vital part of theirs as well. Just as they are helping you construct your life's foundation, you are also helping them to construct theirs. Make your friendships count. Choose your friends wisely and invest in them. Be the kind of friend that they will look back on years later and thank for the way you contributed to their lives.

Be there for your friends in the good times and the bad. Encourage them. Build them up. Motivate them to pursue a great life. It may not be easy. You may have to tell them the truth about a bad choice that they have made or hold them back from doing something they shouldn't, but that's part of being a real friend. Real friends help each other even when the other person doesn't want to be helped.

Places to Go and People to See

Going through high scool creates a type of tunnel vision that reminds me of a horse with blinders on his eyes. Maybe you've seen a horse out in public or in a parade that had these on. It's a device that goes on either side of the horse's head, right beside his eyes. When he is wearing it, he can't see anything around him, only what is directly in front of him.

Many people sacrifice future greatness just to please a couple of people during a few years of school. By doing so, they live such a limited life, as if their friends' opinion of them is all that matters! They, like the horses with blinders, are only looking at what is immediately in front of them.

I have been to graduations where they play the usual "Friends are Friends Forever" song. Everyone holds hands and sings together. It sounds nice (except for that tone deaf guy down in front), and it feels good. After all, you've been friends for a long time now. But in reality, it's quite different than the song would make you believe.

The fact is that almost everyone is going to lose contact with their junior high and high school friends in the years immediately following graduation. So why live for those people when they're going to be gone soon? Most of these teenage friendships are temporary, but their effects can be permanent.

Lasting Influence

I grew up in a small town. I went to the same school with the same kids for 13 years. We only had about 50 people in each grade. I not only knew everyone in my grade but everyone in my high school.

I had some great friends. Some of them were my best friends, and we assumed it would always be that way. But soon after graduation, we began to lose contact. We went separate ways, to different colleges, jobs, and states. It has been over ten years since I graduated, and in all of those years, I've only run into three of the people that I graduated with. Even with all those social networking tools like MySpace or Facebook, I've still only seen three people. We didn't plan it that way, it just happened.

Most teenage friendships are temporary, but their effects can be permanent.

Teenage Construction Zone

The friends you have now, as important as they are, may or may not last you a lifetime. But the decisions they influence you to make will always be a part of your foundation. So many young people sacrifice what they want most in life for what they want right now. They give up their future in order to get temporary pleasures of approval and popularity with a few friends.

The bottom line is that your friends probably won't be around you for too many more years, much less forever. So don't damage your foundation and future on behalf of them. Before long, you will find yourself with a whole new group of friends. That's just the way life is. People will come and go in your life, but the choices that they influence you to make will always be with you.

Please don't get me wrong. While your friends do influence you to some degree, you and you alone are ultimately responsible for the choices that you make. No one plans on becoming an alcoholic, drug addict, divorcee, or spending his or her life in prison. I am sure that was not their goal early in life, but the choices they allowed other people to influence them to make led them in that direction. The earlier you realize that your friends are a major factor in the stability of your life, the better off you will be. Be aware of their power and be careful who you allow on your construction crew!

FRIENDS: THE CONSTRUCTION CREW
WEEK 4

Group Review

Briefly look over last weeks' lesson. In what ways were you challenged to build a better life? Be specific.

"But now I am writing you that you must not associate with anyone who calls himself a brother but is sexually immoral or greedy, an idolater or a slanderer, a drunkard or a swindler. With such a man do not even eat." (1 Corinthians 5:11)

"Do not make friends with a hot-tempered man, do not associate with one easily angered, or you may learn his ways and get yourself ensnared." (Proverbs 22:24-25)

1. Why do you think the Bible warns us not to hang around immoral people?

2. Give an example of this in your life or someone else's life.

Group Discussion

"Don't you know that a little yeast works through
the whole batch of dough?" (1Corinthians 5:6b)

Yeast is used in baking to make the bread rise. A tiny amount is tossed into the dough, yet the effects of it are tremendous. How can you relate yeast to sinful people around you?

"Do not be misled: "Bad company corrupts good
character." (1Corinthians 15:33)

3. Give a specific example of how being around someone caused you to act in a way that you shouldn't have.

Group Discussion

"Do not be yoked together with unbelievers. For
what do righteousness and wickedness have in
common? Or what fellowship can light have
with darkness? ... What does a believer have in
common with an unbeliever?"
(2 Corinthians 6:14-15)

How could allowing unbelievers to be your best friends be dangerous to your Christian walk?

____

____

"I urge you, brothers, to watch out for those who cause divisions and put obstacles in your way that are contrary to the teaching you have learned. Keep away from them. For such people are not serving our Lord Christ, but their own appetites." (Romans 16:17-18a)

4. What does this passage say to do about people who are trying to teach you the wrong way to live?

____

____

"...many live as enemies of the cross of Christ. Their destiny is destruction, their god is their stomach, and their glory is in their shame. Their mind is on earthly things. But our citizenship is in heaven." (Philippians 3:18b-20a)

5. As a Christian you are a ______________ of heaven. Make sure that you don't pick up the lifestyles of those that are just living for what this temporary life has to offer.

"Fear of man will prove to be a snare, but whoever trusts in the Lord is kept safe." (Proverbs 29:25)

"Am I now trying to win the approval of men, or of God? Or am I trying to please men? If I were still trying to please men, I would not be a servant of Christ." (Galatians 1:10)

6. Some people live their lives to please their friends. How do you avoid doing this?

____

____

"And we urge you, brothers, warn those who are idle, encourage the timid, help the weak, be patient with everyone." (1 Thessalonians 5:14)

"A friend loves at all times…" (Proverbs 17:17)

7. Give an example of when being a loving friend might involve some controversy.

____

____

Exercise

Sometimes being a real friend can be hard. Your friend might even get upset, but if you are being obedient to God then you have done the right thing.

Make a list of the five friends that influence you the most. This week pay more attention to how much they influence you.

1. ____________________________________
2. ____________________________________
3. ____________________________________
4. ____________________________________
5. ____________________________________

STANDARDS FOR LIVING

CHAPTER 5

I have learned that the higher a young person's moral standards are, the higher their quality of life. This is because principles observed at a young age usually carry on into adulthood as well. That's why it is so important to think about and define your moral guidelines as early in life as possible.

So, what are morals anyway? A person's morals could be defined as the standard they set for themselves in character, integrity, and purity. I like how the influential English author G.K. Chesterton put it: "Morality, like art, consists in drawing a line somewhere."[2] Without drawing a moral line, you would just do anything and everything with no regard for the repercussions.

When visiting the Grand Canyon Visitation Center, you will notice that there are rails along the rim of the 5,280 ft. deep canyon. The purpose of the rails, obviously, is to keep people from falling over the edge. Likewise, moral lines are also designed to keep you and others from danger. It's a way of setting boundaries in your life that you will not cross.

A person without a moral line is like a ship without a rudder or a car without a steering wheel. That type of living always leads to disaster.

> *The higher your moral standards are, the higher your quality of life will be.*

Moral lines will have to be drawn to encompass a lot of different areas of your life. Basic examples would be your decisions regarding such issues as lying, cheating, and stealing. But sometimes it's a little more complicated.

Are you ok with letting someone cheat off of you during a test? If you disagree with how strictly your parents have grounded you, is it ok to sneak out of the house at night to go see your friends? Will you let your boyfriend or girlfriend take your physical relationship further than you should if it makes them happy? Morals are reflected in what you allow into your body, what you do with your body, and even how you treat others.

Often times, when we make bad choices and lower our moral standards, we immediately think to ourselves: *I wonder if I'll get caught, well at least no one else knows,* or *I sure hope my parents don't find out*. The bottom line is that even if you don't get caught, even if no one else knows, even if your parents don't find out, you really haven't gotten away with anything. Remember how we determined that every choice lays a brick on your foundation? When you make compromising decisions, you have placed those choices, those bricks, on your foundation, and sooner or later, you will feel the effects of those choices.

If you can get through these critical years of your life keeping your morals high, you will have nothing but a foundation of good decisions. A foundation of that strength means that your odds of having a great life will also be incredibly high.

When people begin to lower their moral standard and allow unhealthy decisions to become a part of their life, so goes their chances of having the life that they've dreamed of. You may suffer the consequences in ten seconds, ten days, or ten years down the road. But before long, the consequences of immoral behavior begin to eat away at a person's foundation, their quality of life, and their future.

> **Morals are boundaries in your life that you will not cross; a way of keeping you from danger.**

Keep your standards high! I promise that if you do, you will never get to a point in your life where you regret it. But those who lower their standards, sooner or later, always regret it. *There is nothing and no one worth lowering your moral standards for.* Whatever it is you think you are gaining, it is simply not worth it. Remember, you have to live with you for the rest of your life.

The Power of Peer Pressure

So if we know that keeping our standards high will result in a higher chance of peace, joy, and success, then why do so many young people choose to lower their moral standard anyway? The main reason is the power of peers over a person's good intentions, or in other words, peer pressure.

I know you're probably saying, "Dude, peer pressure? I'm so sick of hearing that phrase!" But hear me out.

You see, the odds are that someday, one of your so-called friends will lower their moral standard in some area. That choice might be taking their first drink or first hit, a sexual experience, or something else. Now that they've made a bad decision, it would just make sense that they would come to you, their friend, to ask for help. But for some strange reason, the opposite usually takes place.

Instead of being apologetic or asking for your help, they will often brag as if what they have done was great. They expect your praise. In reality, they are trying to make their mistakes look like achievements so that they won't have to feel guilty about them. Their choice wasn't really that bad, was it? Don't believe it. By supporting the idea that their mistake was ok, you are giving in to peer pressure.

You just crossed a moral line, made a moral compromise. You just encouraged your friend to do whatever it was, and in the process, you've justified that act in your mind. Now, it's ok for you to share the experience with your friend. I mean, why not? Your friend did it, and they were praised for it. So, after you do that thing that you told yourself you wouldn't do, it's your turn to go to your other friends and (instead of telling them how you feel guilty for lowering your moral standards) brag about that new thing you just did.

> *Never look up to someone who is lowering their moral standards.*

That is why such harmful and unhealthy activities become so popular. As more and more people give in to their friends because they don't want to make them "feel bad," they allow the behavior to continue along the peer pressure chain.

Never look up to someone who is lowering his or her moral standard. Lowering moral standards is easy to do. Don't respect them more because of this. Instead, respect those who have the inner strength to stand their ground and keep their standards high. That is definitely a choice worthy of praise.

If a friend comes to you confessing to an act in a bragging manner, don't approve of it by giving praise or staying silent or laughing along. Be a good friend. Tell them that you don't support their actions. Then explain what you stand for in as humble a tone as possible. Try not to sound judgmental, but let them hear the truth. They may not want to listen, but you have done all that you can do.

The Other Peer Pressure

While most people are aware of the external type of peer pressure that we have been talking about, there is another type of peer pressure that is even more dangerous to your foundation: internal peer pressure. Internal peer pressure is the pressure that we perceive in our minds, but it may not be real at all. It is the pressure that we put on ourselves to fit in or to be accepted.

> *You don't have to change your moral standards to be accepted.*

For instance, think about how contagious bad language can be. When you hear someone cursing, often times you feel the need to talk like them so that they will accept you. Maybe it makes you feel more impressive or confident. But the point is that you are the only one pressuring you to use bad language.

At this stage of your life, your peers will probably put some degree of external peer pressure on you. If you say "no," they will most likely accept you anyway and possibly respect you even more. The real battle is convincing yourself that you don't have to change your moral standards to be accepted.

My freshman year of college, I decided to join a fraternity. During the initiation process, all the freshmen had to drink an entire bottle of champagne while the upper classmen cheered. This is the way that it had always been done. All the freshmen knew that they were expected to do it. So, nine other freshmen initiates that night did exactly that.

However, I had decided long ago that I wasn't going to drink. I met with the frat officers beforehand and shared my standards with them. After hearing my view, they decided to let me drink a bottle of grape juice instead. I was offered alcohol on just a couple of other occasions, but once they realized that I was going to always refuse, they stopped. They didn't even perceive my decision as all that big of a deal, but in my head, the pressure was immense. What would they think? What would they say? Would I be looked down upon? Would I be kicked out of the frat?

Even though they said and thought nothing of the sort, that's what I couldn't stop thinking about. The pressure I was putting on myself was far greater than any pressure they were putting on me. By not letting the internal peer pressure get to me, the external peer pressure also diminished.

> **Every time you overcome pressure, you get a little bit stronger inside.**

Internal peer pressure can be affected by the people and places with which we spend our time, just like external peer pressure. But internal peer pressure has the most to do with what goes on in our very own minds. It's important to realize that you're the one in charge of it. While you cannot always control the external pressure, you do have 100% control over the internal peer pressure that you feel.

Still, just because you have control doesn't mean that overcoming the peer pressure will be easy. Luckily, every time you overcome peer pressure in a situation, you get a little bit stronger inside. It becomes easier and easier to resist the pressure next time. Before long, it will be a piece of cake to make the right choices.

Warning: Moral Line. Do Not Cross!

The best way to avoid becoming a habitually immoral person is to draw your moral lines and never cross them.

Once you do something that crosses your moral boundaries, it will be easier to do it again and again. Before long there is nothing inside of you to hold you back. You have crossed the line so many times that the line is now meaningless to you. It's just like Sissela Bok, a moral philosopher, once said: "It is easy to tell a lie, but hard to tell only one."[3]

I met a guy named Eric at the beginning of my freshmen year of college that made this concept real to me. We arrived at our dormitory the day before school started, and one of the first things he asked me was whether or not I drank. I told him I didn't.

He said that he had never even taken a drink of alcohol in his life and was really going to take a strong stance at college. I was impressed by his boldness and his resolve to influence others in the right direction.

Sadly, his resolve did not last long. After one month, under some pressure from others, he gave in and took his first drink. Making a fool of himself in an all out drunken state quickly became a very normal occurrence for him. After all those years of keeping his line drawn, he moved it, and now that line was long gone. I know that if I had ever given into drinking, even once, I could have been him.

> *Knowing what you believe in is great, but standing for what you believe in is better!*

You have to know what you believe in and be willing to stand strong in your moral convictions. Knowing what you believe in is great, but standing for what you believe in is even better! High morals, integrity, self-control, character, and discipline are vital ingredients to having a joyful life, but in the presence of peer pressure, popularity, and acceptance, many people seem to forget.

Instead of keeping their standards high, they begin to let them slip away. Instead of standing strong for what they know is right, they let whatever is popular at the time determine what their standards should be. The once key ingredients of a joyful life go to the wayside, as they are replaced with strong desires to fit in and feel accepted at any cost.

Creating Your Standards

I want to challenge you to think about your standards and set them as soon as you can. Don't put it off one more day. Sometimes young men and women find themselves surprised by the pressure that has suddenly come upon them.

They haven't thought about what they would do in that type of situation before, and they end up making a decision that they wouldn't have made if they would have had more time to think it through. That's why it's crucial to determine where you stand *before* you have to do so.

What are your standards? To drink or not to drink? Will you try drugs or not? How far will you go with a boyfriend or girlfriend? What kind of music will you listen to? What will you allow yourself to view on the internet? How sexy will you dress? What will you watch on TV? Will you and your friends have conversations about things you know you shouldn't be talking about?

> It's crucial to determine where you stand before you have to make your stand.

As you think about this, remember that you will never look back on your life and say, "I wish my standards in life hadn't been so high." But, I can guarantee you there are many people who say, "I wish I never would have done such and such."

The question is, which one of those people will you be? Where will your moral line be drawn? Will that line be set in concrete or just scribbled on a dry erase board?

Bad Choices Feel So Good!

I understand that just because a choice is bad, doesn't mean that it's not pleasurable. If it didn't feel good, no one would do it. Some people seem to live their lives with the motto of, "If it feels good, do it." However, living your life based on feelings is very dangerous because feelings usually don't take into account the consequences of your decisions. Feelings can be very deceptive and should not be used as our only test of what is right.

It reminds me of the story of a young man who was seeking truth. In his quest, he traveled half way around the world and climbed to the top of the highest mountain in the world to gain wisdom from a very wise philosopher. When he arrived breathless at the top of the mountain, he saw the philosopher sitting on a stone, contemplating the universe. Overwhelmed with joy, he asked the old, wise philosopher the question that had puzzled him for many years.

"Philosopher," he said, "What is right, and what is wrong?" The wise man looked up from where he was seated. The knowledge of a thousand years was reflected in his face.

He graciously stared down his nose at the boy, and said, "What is right for you will feel right to you. What is wrong for you will feel wrong to you."

The young man had the answer that he sought, but it wasn't the answer that he was looking for. Had he really climbed a mountain for this?

After thinking about the answer for a few minutes, he walked closer to the philosopher. He raised up his leg and stomped his hiking boot down on the old man's toes as hard as he could.

"Ouch!" the philosopher cried. "What was that for?!"

The boy said, "It just felt right!"

Some immoral choices that may make us feel pleasure for a moment can bring great displeasure in the future. A drink that leads to a life of alcoholism. A hit of marijuana that leads to a life of addiction. A fit of rage that leads to a life in prison. A single sexual experience that leads to a life of disease.

> *Feelings can be deceptive; instead, cautiously, rationally, and logically think through your decisions.*

As you construct the foundation of your life, don't make your choices based solely on feelings and emotions. Instead, cautiously, rationally, and logically think through your decisions. Many lives are ruined due to one, irrational, quick decision. As you are debating certain activities and choices in your life, I suggest asking yourself a few questions. Ask yourself:

- Will this help my future?
- What would my parents think?
- Would I still approve of this decision in 20 years?
- Could this hurt me or someone else?
- How would I instruct my future kids on this issue?

Though this isn't a complete list, you get the point. If you take time to consider your choices and not just base them on a momentary feeling, you will make choices that will become strong bricks and add vital strength to your life's foundation.

Everybody Makes Mistakes!

Nobody is perfect. Every human on the planet makes mistakes, but remember failing is not falling, but failing to rise after you have fallen. If you have lowered your moral standards already, I am not trying to rag on you or make you feel hopeless. I want to encourage you to stand up, raise your boundaries back up, and keep trying. It's going to be harder now that you have crossed your moral boundaries, but it isn't impossible.

> *Failing is not falling, but failing to rise after you have fallen.*

One of my best friends is a guy who spent three years in prison. In high school, he started messing around with drugs. When he began to lower his morals, his entire life soon followed. He turned into an addict, a total mess. He sold drugs just to buy his own. He made some horrible decisions, and he paid the price.

However, he didn't allow those mistakes to take him down forever. While in prison, he did some serious thinking. He acknowledged his mistakes and began to take action to change who he had become. During that time he changed his life, renewed his moral boundaries, and came out a different man.

If you have messed up, get back up before the dust even settles. People that stay down too long seem to get used to it, and after a while, they don't mind it anymore.

Avoid falling morally at all cost. But if you do fall, get

back up, shake it off, learn from it, and do what it takes to avoid it from happening again! Don't use your fall as an excuse to stay down and just keep making bad choices. Stop immediately, and get back on track!

Success is Up to You!

I am meeting more and more young people today who understand the value of setting and maintaining these higher standards for themselves. Is it easy? Of course not! Is it possible? Absolutely!

I understand that it is easy to just go with the flow. It is much more difficult to say no and go against the flow. Anyone can get drunk, anyone can do drugs, and anyone can have sex. In order to take a stand, you have to learn to be not only present minded, but future minded as well.

> *Make decisions because they're right, not just popular.*

I went all the way through school without ever taking a drink of alcohol, smoking, taking drugs, or having sex. I'm not bragging or patting myself on the back. I'm just letting you know that it is possible. With the right mind set it can be done!

Always be thinking about the repercussions of your decisions. Try to constantly remind yourself that your present life and future success depend on the choices you place on your foundation now. Don't make your decisions just because they're popular, but because they're right.

Even if your entire school voted that taking drugs was the right thing to do, would that make it ok? Of course not! Remember, people come and go, but the choices that you make are always with you. Set your standards high, begin to draw the line, and say no to things that are not beneficial to your future.

STANDARDS FOR LIVING
WEEK 5

Group Review

Briefly look over last weeks' lesson. Did you try to be more aware of the how your friends influenced you? Think of an example where a friend influenced you to do, say, dress, or act a certain way.

> "But the fruit of the Spirit is love, joy, peace, patience, kindness, goodness, faithfulness, gentleness and self-control. Against such things there is no law. Those who belong to Christ Jesus have crucified the sinful nature with its passions and desires."
> (Galatians 5:22-24)

1. What are other types of behavior that should be found in a Child of God? What do these fruits look like in day to day life?

____

____

> "Do not conform any longer to the pattern of this world, but be transformed by the renewing of your mind. Then you will be able to test and approve what God's will is—his good, pleasing and perfect will." (Romans 12:2)

2. Is it easier for you to be conformed to the world's standards, or transform to God's standards? ___________

Explain why.

____

____

____

Group Discussion

Conforming to our surroundings is virtually automatic, unless we take intentional steps to keep it from happening. What are some practical real life things that we can do to continue transforming into who God wants us to be and not conforming to who the world wants us to be?

____

____

"Flee the evil desires of youth, and pursue righteousness, faith, love and peace, along with those who call on the Lord out of a pure heart." (2 Timothy 2:22)

3. Evil desires are very common. As teenagers these desires can seem even more appealing, but this verse says to _______ from them. Not only are we supposed to do this, but we are to _______________ righteousness, faith, love, and peace as well. The easiest way to get away from evil is to pursue good.

"Let your eyes look straight ahead, fix your gaze directly before you. Make level paths for your feet and take only ways that are firm. Do not swerve to the right or the left; keep your foot from evil." (Proverbs 4:26-27)

4. Walking with God means staying focused on what he would have you do. It's easy to swerve off the road when you're not looking straight ahead. What are some things or people that have caused you to swerve or want to swerve?

____

____

Group Discussion

"Test everything. Hold on to the good. Avoid every kind of evil." (1 Thessalonians 5:21-22)

How should we test everything?

____

____

"He whose walk is blameless is kept safe, but he whose ways are perverse will suddenly fall." (Proverbs 28:18)

5. People fall or thrive based upon their standards for living. According to this verse if you are ______________ you are kept safe, but if you are _______________ you will fall.

Exercise

This chapter was about setting your morals and standards. Find some time this week and do some serious thinking about what your morals and standards are going to be. Make sure to use the word of God, and the example of Godly people in your life to establish them.

FOUNDATION BREAKERS: DRUGS AND ALCOHOL

CHAPTER 6

The commitment I made in high school not to drink alcohol or do drugs was strengthened even further when I went to college. I know that might sound weird since so many people seem to use that extra freedom to party hard.

In high school, you can look around and see a few people who are starting to reap the negative consequences of their decisions to allow drugs and alcohol into their life.

At college, hardly a day goes by that you don't hear of someone getting kicked out of school, arrested, in a wreck, or even date raped due to the power of alcohol or drugs. That gave me more reasons to make my moral stance even stronger.

I witnessed many students with a potentially great future have to leave school after the first semester. It wasn't because they weren't smart enough, but because they let drugs and alcohol into their lives. They lost control.

Most of them had already given in to one or the other in

high school, but the unchecked freedom they had in college helped them feed these cravings like never before. Some would lose out on an education, a career, or even more. They were willing to give up their dreams, goals, and future just to have a good time. I know that you will save yourself a world of hurt by never letting alcohol into your life.

Don't give up on your dreams, goals, and future just to have a good time right now.

I received a call from a friend of mine last week. He told me that his Dad was in the hospital and didn't have long to live. His Dad's liver was only operating at 10%, and his kidneys were shutting down completely. My friend was not surprised at all. In fact, he was amazed that his dad had lived this long.

His father had been an alcoholic for over thirty years. For years, his family had witnessed alcohol consume his dad's life. Every day of his dad's life became one more rush to get drunk. It had destroyed his dad as a husband, a father, and a human; and now it was stealing away his wasted life. The alcohol he had consumed finally consumed him.

Have you ever noticed how the end result of alcoholism is perceived completely differently than the beginning of alcoholism? For example, the school drunk is probably one of the most popular guys in high school. But if you could fast forward time and get a glimpse of his life in twenty, thirty, or forty years, you would see a totally different guy.

Studies show that you would probably see him reaping consequences like unemployment, divorce, disease, homelessness, depression, and jail or prison time. He would be held hostage by his addictions. His life would be wasted, his goals not attained. His dreams would always be just dreams. All sacrificed at the bottom of the bottle.

The only reason people think the school drunk is cool is because they haven't seen the end result of his choices. If what you see now is a guy who's a little rebellious, crazy, and a whole lot of fun to laugh at, just wait. The foundation that he is constructing is built for disaster.

Some will think that just one drink can't hurt, that they're not going to get drunk or they'll just have one or two. Don't deceive yourself! Even if you think it's just going to be one time, the decision to drink is a very serious and dangerous brick to place on your foundation. It will have far reaching repercussions.

> *Not doing something the first time is the best way to avoid doing it again.*

One drink is how every alcoholic began his or her journey down hill. Not doing something for the first time is the best way to avoid doing it again. When you take that first drink, you have justified in your mind that it is ok this time, which logically will make it ok for next time. At first, you may try to limit drinking to special occasions or parties. Before long you will start to find more and more "special occasions," until there isn't a need for an occasion because it has become a way of life.

Most people don't realize they're addicted until it's too late. While I will talk briefly about drugs, alcohol is the topic that I am going to spend most of my time on, because it, by far, is the most abused substance amongst teenagers. I truly believe that if you can learn to resist allowing alcohol into your life, then resisting drugs will not be a problem.

> *Most people don't realize they're addicted until it's too late.*

While certain percentages of young people will try crack, ecstasy, marijuana or heroin, almost 80% of graduating high school seniors will have consumed alcohol. So what are the consequences of all this drinking?

- Drunk driving is the number one cause of death amongst teenagers.[4]
- An American dies every twenty minutes from an alcohol related car crash.[5]
- Alcohol kills 6.5 times more young people than all other illicit drugs combined.[6]
- Youth who drink alcohol are 16 times more likely to use other illegal drugs.[7]
- Young people who drink are more likely to be victims of violent crimes, including rape.[8]

- 40% of people who start drinking before the age of 15 will eventually become alcoholics.[9]
- Alcohol is linked with teenage deaths by drowning, fire, suicide and homicide.[10]
- Over 15 million people in America are alcohol abusers or alcoholics.[11]
- More than 4,000 young people die each year as a result of alcohol poisoning.[12]

In view of these facts, why would anyone ever decide to allow alcohol into their lives? It is illogical, irrational, unhealthy, and risky to say the least. Anyone in the right frame of mind would easily see that the risks are not worth the payoff. The cost far outweighs the benefit.

A Matter of Life and Death

About four years ago, I was standing in the middle of a high school gym floor talking to 400 students about the consequences of placing alcohol on your foundation. I noticed that several seniors were visibly upset. One of the school counselors saw the students and made her way to them. She tried her best to console them while everyone else stared. You know how it is.

As the assembly ended, I asked one of the principals what had happened. Apparently, three very popular high school boys had left a party two months earlier. They had all been drinking, but they thought they could make it home anyway.

The alcohol slowed the response time of the driver. He lost control of the car as he was going around a corner. The police said he was killed immediately. The front seat passenger was seriously injured but still alive.

The young man in the back seat wasn't hurt at all. As he stumbled out of the car, his friend screamed at him to go get help. The boy in the back seat tried to get help, staggering down the road, but he soon passed out. Not because he was injured, but because he was so drunk.

> *You may think that there are good reasons to try alcohol, but none are worth the risk.*

When he regained consciousness, the fire trucks were trying to put out the flames engulfing the car. His friend was still inside. Both of the boys in the front seat died that night. That day, the survivor was in the assembly.

The entire town witnessed firsthand the destructive power of alcohol. Those young men never intended such a horrific accident to happen. They were just out to have a "good time." But at what price? In a heartbeat, that "good time" turned into total catastrophe. It didn't happen when their car slammed into the tree. It happened when they decided to have their first drink.

When you play with something as powerful as alcohol, events can quickly spiral out of control. As horrible as this story is, it's just one of the several thousand similar alcohol related accidents that happen every year amongst teenagers.

Even in the face of devastating stories and knowing the possible effects of adding alcohol to their lives, many young people still choose it. Some of them will try it because of curiosity, rebellion, popularity, or because they like the high. In many circles, it's even a sign of prestige and respect.

But know this: while you may think there are good reasons to try alcohol, none of them are worth the risk.

Addiction

I know a married man in his late thirties with a wife and two beautiful little girls. He battles a drug addiction that started years ago during high school. He owns his own business, but he can't be trusted with the finances. His wife gives him twenty dollars a day, enough for lunch and gas money, because that's all he can be trusted with. He's not allowed to have any credit cards or cash, because if he does, he will be tempted to buy drugs.

About two months ago, he secretly got a credit card for his business. He immediately racked up $6,000 worth of debt, all of which was used for recreational drugs. For two weeks he was gone, high, and out of control. When the money ran out, he finally returned home.

Everything was a wreck. His business suffered, his family suffered. Trust between he and his spouse was destroyed. His little girls couldn't figure out why Daddy was acting so strange. He laid in bed for days nauseous, shivering, and throwing up, waiting for the drugs to totally leave his body.

He is the sole bread winner for his family. While he spent $6,000 on drugs, his wife didn't even have enough money in the house to buy groceries for the kids to eat. I bet he never thought that what he did in high school would still be haunting him years later. This has been the norm for many years now: promises to change, followed by episodes of serious drug abuse, and then disaster.

Drugs are very powerful and highly addictive. Once they enter a person's body, they quickly take control of the person's entire life. Some people become so addicted, they will do anything to get more. A drug addict may sell every possession, turn to prostitution, steal, or even kill if they think it will get them the drug. Our prison system is packed with inmates, the majority of which are there due to drug related offenses.

> Once drugs enter your body, they quickly take control.

There are many people who are walking around amongst us who use, abuse, or are addicted to drugs. They may not be in a state or federal prison yet, but they are in a self-made prison. They are contained by the walls of addiction. The drugs control their every thought and action. Lives, families, and jobs are lost daily from the effects of drugs in peoples' lives. Most of these addicts started their experimentation during their teenage years. What started as "fun," "recreational," or "partying" now controls their very existence.

How can you know if that one experimental drug use or drink of alcohol will lead to an addiction? How will you know if your life will be destroyed by these foundation breakers?

There's only one way to know for sure. If you don't take your first drink, you will never be an alcoholic! If you don't smoke your first cigarette, you will never be addicted to smoking! You will never ever be addicted to drugs, if you never try them.

There is only one way to assure that you will not be affected by these addictive substances, and that is by totally and completely keeping them out of your life. According to the president of the National Center on Addiction and Substance Abuse, "A child who reaches age 21 without smoking, abusing alcohol, or using drugs is virtually certain not to do so."[13]

> *You don't need to know every drug out there, just your reason to reject them all.*

Lasting Effects

Alcohol, cigarettes, recreational drugs, and prescription drugs are all used to get a temporary high that can lead to a lifetime of lows. The effects may or may not be immediate, but the damage adds up. Take something like cigarettes for example. The Center for Disease Control says that millions of people die prematurely because of the effects of smoking cigarettes.[14]

Cigarettes have over 40 different carcinogens (cancer causing agents) in them. Marijuana has 50-70% more cancer causing agents than cigarettes, and these are two substances that many young people consider virtually harmless.[15] Other "harder" drugs are even more harmful. They can quickly cause permanent damage to the mind or body. Many of these have the power to cause addiction after only one try.

This book is not designed to be an exhaustive resource about specific drugs and their effects. It is designed to help you understand why you should not allow any of them on your life's foundation. No matter what the drug or its side effects are, you don't have to worry about it if you never try it.

> *You can't abuse your body and then get a new one at Wal-mart.*

You don't need to know about every drug out there. All you need to know is your reasons for rejecting all of them. I believe that any young person who rationally and objectively weighs out the risk will understand that experimentation with drugs or alcohol is just not worth it.

Learn to treat your body with care and respect, because it's the only one you've got! You only have one mind and one body, and how you treat it now greatly effects how it will work later on.

Some people act as if they can abuse their bodies and then

take it back to Wal-Mart for another one. But what you do to your body stays with you until the day you die.

I cannot promise that if you keep drugs, alcohol, and cigarettes out of your body, you will be healthy enough to play soccer with your great-great grandkids when you're a 120 years old. But, I can promise you that you will be a lot closer to living a long, wonderful, and fulfilled life if you protect your mind and body from these dangerous substances. While you cannot control everything in life, you can absolutely control what comes into your body. It is the vessel that you have been given to live out this life, so take care of it.

Scooping Fire and Playing with Snakes

Can you just have a little drink every now and then or just an occasional hit of marijuana and still be ok? There is an ancient proverb that asks the question, "Can a man scoop fire into his lap and not get burned?"

Obviously it's a rhetorical question. Of course you can't! Don't expect to play with fire and not get burned.

It's sort of like the man in India who had a pet Cobra. He raised it from a little snake, took care of it, fed it and loved it, but one day the Cobra bit him. The man was shocked by the incident. As he lay dying, he couldn't understand why the cobra had bitten him. He just didn't get it.

You would never put fire in your lap on purpose or make a deadly Cobra your pet. But when young people allow alcohol or drugs into their lives, they are trying to play with something that's just as destructive. They are taking a gamble with their lives, and they will lose. No matter why they do it, it's not worth the damage that it causes.

Let me make this clear: alcohol and drugs only bring weakness to your foundation. They cannot do anything to add strength. If you truly want to have a great life, then hold on to it. Don't risk losing everything that you've built by using alcohol or drugs.

> Don't risk losing everything you've built by using drugs or alcohol.

People with the strength to continually keep these things out of their life are incredibly rare. Others may not understand, and may even mock you because of your view. But even if they don't immediately respect your decision, in time they definitely will.

Tip: Avoid Bad by Pursuing Good

A great life is not just about the absence of negative choices, but the presence of positive choices as well. Don't focus on what you can't do. By trying not to think about something, you are still thinking about it. Instead, focus on actively pursuing a goal with great passion. Hands that are busy doing good don't have time to do bad.

Get involved in something that interests you and pursue it. Studies have shown that teens with less time to just hang out doing nothing are less likely to be involved in high risk behavior. Not because they are necessarily trying to avoid it, but because they are so busy making constructive decisions that they don't have the time to make destructive foundation breaking decisions.

Whether it is sports, music, a band, writing, art, church, martial arts, games, volunteering, poetry, or whatever you like, get involved and stay active. It will benefit you beyond just helping you avoid foundation breakers. You will also develop strong friendships, focus, commitment, and discipline.

If you don't know what type of activity to pursue, I suggest looking over your own words. Take a look at what you wrote down for the Goal Exercise portion of this book. Start pursuing those goals, dreams, accomplishments, and attributes that you listed. There is no time like the present to start taking charge of your foundation and your future. Don't put off until tomorrow the good that you can do today.

FOUNDATION BREAKERS: DRUGS AND ALCOHOL
WEEK 6

Group Review

Last week's lesson talked about peer pressure. Did you witness peer pressure taking place in your life or anyone else's life. Think of an example to share.

"Wine is a mocker and beer a brawler; whoever is led astray by them is not wise." (Proverbs 20:1)

1. Anyone who is "led astray" by alcohol is not __________.

"Do not get drunk on wine, which leads to debauchery. Instead, be filled with the Spirit." (Ephesians 5:18)

2. Anything such as alcohol or drugs can easily lead to all types of sin. Instead of being filled and controlled by such substances, we as Christians are to be filled and controlled by the ____________________.

Group Discussion

Just because the Bible doesn't mention specific substances like drugs and cigarettes, is it okay for us to do it? Why or why not?

"For he chose us in him before the creation of the world to be holy and blameless in his sight." (Ephesians 1:4)

3. Is it enough to be blameless in our friends' or even parents' sight? It is important to understand that God sees everything we do and everything we think. Our goal should not be to just be blameless in people's eyes but in the eyes of God.

4. Analyze your own life. Have you put proper boundaries up between you and foundation breakers? If not, do some serious thinking about setting boundaries up that God would be proud of.

"No temptation has seized you except what is common to man. And God is faithful; he will not let you be tempted beyond what you can bear. But when you are tempted, he will also provide a way out so that you can stand up under it." (1 Corinthians 10:13)

5. What are some things in your life that help you resist sin? Be specific.

____

____

____

Group Discussion

"I applied my heart to what I observed and learned a lesson from what I saw" (Proverbs 24:32)

Do you think the people you hang around could be an influence on how often you are tempted by alcohol or drugs?

____

Exercise

If you are currently using alcohol or drugs, make it your goal this week to stop and to get someone to help you stop.

If you are tempted to use alcohol and drugs, figure out what that temptation is and think about a way to cut it out of your life this week.

If you are not currently in an environment that makes you feel tempted to try alcohol or drugs, think up some ways to protect yourself if the temptation ever arises.

SEX AND EFFECTS

CHAPTER 7

Premarital sex is glamorized by television shows, movies, musicians and magazines. It is so prevalent that most teenagers seem to accept that it's expected of them as well. However, these media outlets rarely show the consequences that premarital sex plays in a person's life.

The media conveniently leaves out the sexually transmitted diseases, pregnancies, sterility, abortions, increased chance of future divorce, eighteen years of child support, and psychological damage. Instead, they only show the pleasure of the sexual moment. Sexual desires can be powerful, and the media may make premarital sex out to be normal. But you must remember that your goal is not to just be "normal," your goal is to be great!

There is no doubt that your attitude and choices regarding sexual matters are going to be very influential bricks on your life's foundation. These bricks have the power to change a person's whole life. I have presented real stories of real people in this chapter to show that there are serious, and potentially dangerous, consequences to having premarital sex. My purpose is not to scare you into making the right decision. I simply want you to think about the consequences of the choices that you will be faced with.

> *Your goal is not to just be "normal," your goal is to be great!*

Getting More Than You Expected

After I had finished speaking at a high school in Arkansas, a teenage girl approached me. She told me that I was right. Not knowing what she meant by that, I asked her to explain.

She told me that in two days she was going to have a surgery to remove her cervix. The doctor told her that she had developed cervical cancer from a sexually transmitted disease.

She said, "My decision to have sex has now cost me the ability to ever have children."

While some young people who make high risk sexual decisions don't suffer the consequences of their choices for many years, the consequences of her actions were virtually immediate. I talked with her for quite some time. She had come face to face with the repercussions of her high risk behavior.

Since then, she had decided to be abstinent and was making every effort to raise her moral standards. But, the fact of the matter is that her life is forever changed, all because of the bricks she chose to put on the foundation of her life during her sophomore year.

Often, the consequences of being sexually active are not even thought about in a rush to fulfill sexual desires. As a result, there are over 18.9 million new cases of sexually transmitted diseases each year. Close to half of these cases are developed in people between the ages of 15 and 24.[16] These people usually pass the disease on to everyone that they are intimate with in the future, including their eventual spouse.

Imagine the pain of giving a disease that you got from someone else to the person you love most. What makes it worse is that many of the diseases are not curable. Some people have to live with a sexually transmitted disease for the rest of their lives, all due to choices made during their foundational years.

Diseases are contagious. Even if you've had sex with only one person, you are in effect having sex with everyone they have ever had sex with, and everyone that those people have had sex with, and everyone that those people have had sex with. And it keeps going.

> *One sexual encounter can put you at risk of catching something from hundreds of people.*

Think about it. One sexual encounter could put you at risk of catching something from dozens or even hundreds of other people.

It Won't Happen to Me

Before I was about to speak at a school assembly in Texas, I was chatting with the principal.

In an attempt to prepare me for my talk, he told me, "Just so you know, there are going to be five pregnant girls in your audience today."

"Well, that's about the national average for a high school," I told him.

The principal shuffled his feet and said, "You don't understand. The high school is down the road. This is the middle school."

Wow! That took me by surprise.

After the assembly was over, I had a moment to sit down and speak with each of the pregnant girls. I found out that none of them were still with the father of their babies. Each girl took a few minutes to tell me a little of their story.

One girl said that her boyfriend was constantly pressuring her; another told of how her boyfriend had said, "If you love me, then you'll let me."

One by one, they had all rationalized the decision to have sex, and now they were reaping the consequences. Even though their stories were all a little different, they had one common thread. They each told me of how they never thought that something like this could happen to them.

I seem to see this attitude with a lot of young men and

women. They listen to school speakers, read books, or hear statistics of the consequences of sexual behavior, but they think, just like those young ladies did, that it won't happen to them. Little do they realize, they are exactly the people whom "it" will happen to.

The only way that "it" will not happen to you is if you do not put the choice of sex before marriage on your foundation. You see, you can't get pregnant, or get someone pregnant, if you don't have sex! It's that simple!

A Horrible Dilemma

I never will forget the dilemma that an 11th grade young lady was facing at a school in Florida. When I had finished speaking at the assembly, the other students all began to go back to class.

However, this one girl made her way, against the flow of people, to me. She stopped just in front of me and turned to look back, as if to see if someone was watching her. She told me that her boyfriend had just given her the money to have an abortion, but she wanted my opinion on the matter.

Her bluntness left me speechless. She stood there staring at me, waiting to hear what I would say. I gathered myself and told her what I believed. I told her that having an abortion is not just a little decision you make and then go on with life like nothing ever happened. It's a decision that has lasting consequences which some women never heal from.

I let her know that just because you make one mistake,

doesn't mean that you should make another.

I wanted to tell her about all the physical and psychological effects of having an abortion, but within seconds the bell rang, and off to class she went.

I had no idea that I would face such a serious question and have only a matter of seconds to answer it. I think about that young lady often. She was clearly worried and distraught. If only she had waited, she wouldn't have found herself in this situation. But for whatever reason, she decided to have sex outside of marriage.

I can only hope that she made the right decision that day. She had made a choice, placed a brick on her foundation, and was already reaping the consequences.

She is not alone in her dilemma. In the United States, there are almost 1,000,000 teenage pregnancies a year.[17] One thing I always hear from these young mothers is that they wish they knew then what they know now. Almost all of them wish they could go back and change their decision to have sex. Young girls who should be enjoying their teenage years hanging out with friends are suddenly thrust into making some very adult decisions.

> *Almost all pregnant teenagers wish they could go back and change their decision to have sex.*

Some of these young mothers will choose to raise their babies or give them up for adoption. Sadly, some of these women will abort their babies. The fact of the matter is that none of their lives will never be the same again.

Blinded by Love

Usually when you are in a relationship for a long time, you begin to attach your emotional strings to that person. Often, you overlook actions that would normally raise a red flag because the feelings of love have blinded you. You've probably heard the saying "love is blind."

> *Feeling in love will often cause you to overlook actions that would normally raise a red flag.*

That's truer than you know. It is very common that as a relationship builds, young people start thinking and making their decisions based only on their emotions. Young people who decide to get involved sexually magnify that emotional attachment and "love is blind" attitude to a far greater level.

Many people often overlook obvious bad behavior, such as abuse, anger, drinking, lying, flirting with others, and even unfaithfulness, because they have gone all the way with someone. They feel like they are in love.

Some are totally deceived into thinking that "this is the one" just because they have had sex. Others know good and well that this is not "the one," but they still try to make it work to protect their self-image. They don't want to believe that they just gave themselves away to someone they will not always be with. Colleen Kelly Mast, author of Sex Respect, writes: "Because sex is so powerful, it creates very strong emotional bonds between partners. These bonds can make us believe a relationship is deeper than it really is, that we know our partners much better than we actually do."[18]

When teenagers do give in and have sex, it tends to become an all consuming drive. Instead of getting to know a person for who they really are, they become virtually controlled by the desire to have more sex together. They become much more likely to settle for the "wrong person," just because they've had sex. If young people put their sexual desires on hold, they find that they are free to explore who the person truly is and develop relationship skills that will be beneficial throughout life.

Divorce? I'm Not Even Married!

Studies show that one out of two young people in high school are living with only one of their birth parents.[19] Most of them have parents who have been divorced at least once. If I were to ask those students what they wanted their future to look like, I guarantee you they wouldn't mention incessant fighting and heartache, spending a lot of time and money in court, having to pay child support, or forcing their children to decide if they want to live with mom or dad. Sadly, many of them are unwittingly laying their foundation for divorce.

Sexual promiscuity – fooling around sexually – is one of the leading causes for divorce. Young people that go through their teenage years sleeping with multiple partners have a much higher rate of divorce later in life.[20] They cheapen sex during their foundational years by not waiting. Once they eventually marry and try to stay faithful, more often than not, they resort back to the habits they formed as a teenager.

> **Teenagers who sleep with multiple partners run a higher risk of getting a divorce.**

By waiting until marriage to have sex, everyone wins – you, your spouse, and your kids. It is hard to believe, but the bricks you place on your foundation involving sex have the power to influence more of your future than you can even imagine, so choose wisely!

Why Wait?

While sexuality out of control is a very destructive force, sexuality in the boundaries of marriage can be very constructive. It can lead to a deeper marriage relationship. Those who wait are much more likely to be fulfilled and satisfied with their marriage and their spouse. Their marriage will be more stable, trust will be higher, and they will have the peace of mind that neither of them has ever been with anyone else.

A young person's chance of actually saving themselves for marriage is much higher if they can see the reasons not to have sex, along with the benefits of waiting. Some of the benefits of waiting include:

- No risk of giving a sexually transmitted disease to your future spouse.

- Not having to deal with the guilt or resentment that comes from you or your spouse having multiple partners.
- More value placed upon sex within your marriage.[22]
- More self-discipline in other areas of your life because you have learned how to exercise discipline over your sexual life.
- Lower chance of divorce.[23]
- Becoming a positive role model for others and your future children.
- Greater trust in your marriage. If your spouse knows that you were able to resist premarital sex, then they know that you can resist extramarital sex.
- The incomparable peace of having a clear conscience.
- The ability to still be friends with a boyfriend or girlfriend, even if you stop dating.

Your stance on sexual issues will become an important part of your foundation. How a person thinks and acts sexually during their foundational years greatly affects their future.

Virgin!

A great friend of mine and fellow motivational speaker was talking to 2,000 high school students in Georgia on the issue of sex. As he was speaking, a 9th grade girl acknowledged that she was still a virgin. Many people began in the assembly started to laugh at her. In particular, there was a group of older girls who really started making fun of her.

The girl gathered herself, looked them in the eye, and said, "You can laugh all you want, but in reality, I'm more of a lady than you. I can be like you anytime, but you will never be like me again."

Everyone around her got very quiet. The tide had reversed, and the students even began applauding her for her resolve to wait.

You see, she wasn't concerned about what other people might say, her popularity, or who might not go out with her now. She knew that she was making the right decision, and she stood up for it. Stand up for what is right, even if you have to stand alone.

That 9th grade girl will never regret her choice to stay pure until marriage, but those other girls, who were laughing at her, will regret their choice to be promiscuous. The love they think they've earned from their sexual promiscuity isn't love at all. The popularity that they have worked so hard to attain will one day vanish. All they will be left with is the negative ramifications of their decisions. They will carry all their sexual baggage into their marriage. Those girls have made their choices and constructed a foundation, but it is not the kind that will support a strong marriage.

Stand up for what is right, even if you have to stand alone.

However, the girl who stood up for what is right realized

that her purity is one of the greatest treasures that she could ever give to her spouse. Later in life when she marries, she and her husband will have a relationship unscathed by emotional scars, baggage or disease. They will truly understand that the word *virgin* is not a put down, but a virtue. It is something to be treasured, honored, and kept for your spouse. Since they remained pure through their foundational years, they have added amazing strength to their foundation. This type of construction is one that will support a strong, gratifying, and lasting marriage.

If you are a virgin, male or female, you have nothing to be ashamed of and no reason to be embarrassed. Some people think that they are better than you because they've had sex, but in reality, anyone can have sex. There's nothing impressive about that. Sixty-seven percent of surveyed teens who have had sexual intercourse wish they had waited longer.

> **If you are a virgin, male or female, there is no reason to be ashamed or embarrassed.**

It's easy to give in to sexual desires. If you wanted to, you could have sex with someone. Will that make you somehow more of a man or more of a lady? Of course not, but that's what some illogical peers will try to tell you. Don't worry about taking advice from those who are already doing a poor job with their own foundation.

I know a guy who got married three years ago at 34 years old. He was still a virgin. I know it's hard to believe, but it's true. You might be thinking that he must have been some kind of geek that looked like Shrek to remain a virgin that long. But this guy was six feet seven inches tall, 280 lbs., star football player, an All-American wrestler, and played college football.

The point is that you don't have to believe the virgin stereotype that others try to cast. Virgins aren't social outcast, or abnormal people. They are just people who are determined to control their bodies, and not let their bodies control them. In general, they are people who are willing to make a sacrifice now in order to build the strongest life possible. When I meet a young man or woman who admits to being a virgin, I immediately know that I am in the presence of someone whose foundation is unshakeable.

If Not Now, Then When?

Walking through the airport, a magazine cover in the window of a store caught my eye. It said in big print: "When are you ready?"

The article was about how young people know when they are ready to have sex. The writer of the article had interviewed teenagers and gotten their opinion on the matter.

Some teenagers said that a person was ready at a certain age or after they had dated someone for so long. Others said that a person was ready when they knew that they were in love. My favorite, though, was the really deep one: "You'll be ready when you know that you are ready." Could you be a little more specific?

The answers were all so varied and vague. Their "solutions" could easily do more damage than good. It made me realize that there are a lot of young people looking for the answer to that question.

Well, if you don't mind, I think I can bring some clarity to the matter. You see, you are not ready to have sex when you reach a magical age, when you've been dating someone for a while, when you feel like it, or even when you think you love someone.

You are ready to make that decision when you exchange rings with your future spouse. When you commit to love, cherish, and be with that person for a lifetime, that is when you are truly ready! The benefits of a sexual relationship should come only when you and that special someone have committed to be with each other for a lifetime. Marriage is the proof that you are ready.

I've Gone Too Far! Now What?

> *Marriage is the proof that you are ready to have sex.*

I am not ignorant of the fact that many people reading this book are no longer virgins. If that's you, you might be thinking that there is nothing left for you to do except wait for all of the negative consequences to hit you upside the head. It's simply not true. I don't want you to think that it's too late to change. It's never too late to start making the right choices.

If you have made sexual mistakes, don't keep making them because you think it's too late for you. Just because you've made one mistake doesn't justify making more.

Let's pretend that you are driving to a friend's house 30 miles away. What would you do if after traveling 10 miles, you realized that you were going the wrong direction? Would you just keep going the wrong direction? Of course not. You would turn around and go the right way.

Yes, your mistake caused you to waste twenty minutes of your day. But if you would have kept going the wrong way, it would have cost you hours or days depending on how far you kept going.

So it is with sexual mistakes. If you have messed up, then don't keep going the wrong way. You may have to reap the consequence of your mistakes, but that's no reason to keep going and pay an even bigger price. Just because you've placed one bad brick on your foundation, doesn't mean you should start building a whole foundation of bad bricks.

Stop. Turn around, and start doing everything you can do to get back on track! I know this is easier said than done, but it will be worth it!

You can't change the past. What's done is done. The first step now is to admit that it was wrong. Analyze why it happened and take the steps to prevent it from happening again.

If you are currently in a sexual relationship, I would suggest taking an immediate break from the relationship. Take at least a month to get your mind clear. Let your partner know that you believe it was wrong and see what they think about the situation. I know it will be difficult, but you may need to break up with the person.

It's important to be even more intentional in avoiding people and places that could make it easy for you to make the same mistake again. You will have to set strict rules for yourself, who you date, and where you date.

Many teenagers struggle with feelings of tremendous guilt after giving themselves away sexually. They sometimes feel that they are not as valuable as they once were. I want you to know that you are still just as valuable! You are important, and you have a whole life ahead of you.

I remember a teacher in 7th grade who told me that having a pity party is okay, as long as you put a time limit on it. Guilt is only good for a short time. It can help you learn from mistakes, but continually allowing guilt to control our lives is just not healthy.

Sexual Abuse

If you have been sexually abused, molested, or raped, you are in an entirely different situation. Like all other types of abuse, what has happened to you is not your fault. Let someone you can trust know about it. Whatever you do, don't act like nothing has happened.

Sexual abuse brings more than just guilt; it hurts physically, emotionally, mentally, and spiritually. Part of placing good bricks on your foundation is getting help with things that you can't do by yourself. This not only means help in dealing emotionally with past abusive experiences, but getting help to stop continuing abuse. Do not allow it to keep happening.

Taking Responsibility

Bryce was a 17 year old rebel without a cause. He was constantly playing the party animal role. Everything changed after a party one night when he wrecked his car. Due to the wreck, he lost many of his abilities in his upper body and was paralyzed from the waist down. As he lay in the hospital trying to cope with the fact that he would never walk again, his was informed that his girlfriend was several months pregnant and didn't want the baby.

Over the next few weeks, this "party animal" did a lot of thinking. He realized that he had made some mistakes in life, but he took ownership for his choices. He decided to raise the baby himself, even though he was partially paralyzed.

Bryce's accident happened over 15 years ago. The last time I talked with Bryce, I couldn't help but try to imagine how difficult it must have been for him as a teenage boy to take on the responsibility of raising a baby by himself while learning to cope with the severe limitations of his disability. But what made it even more real was when I saw his beautiful

15 year old daughter enter the room to ask him a question.

His life struggles and achievements could easily fill this entire book, but the one point that I want to leave you with is that, despite everything, he kept the baby. He could have easily thought that raising a child would be too difficult, inconvenient, or even impossible, but he accepted the challenge and went on to raise an amazing young lady. He fully accepted the responsibility of raising the life that he helped create.

If Bryce could do it under those circumstances, then I believe that no one has an excuse. He knew that he had made mistakes, but he did everything he could to make them right.

Helpful Advice to Avoid Sexual Mistakes!

1. Wrong Place

Don't set yourself up for failure by finding yourself in the wrong place. It seems all too common to hear about two teenagers who did not plan on having sex, but gave in because they spent time together at the wrong places, such as when two teens find themselves all alone in a parked car or alone in a house with no one around.

> Wrong Place
> + Wrong People
> + Wrong Mindset
> = Wrong Choices

The best way to avoid this from happening is to never be completely alone with your boyfriend or girlfriend! I know that sounds painful and even extreme at first, but the more privacy young couples have, the more prone they are to give in to sexual desires.

Make sure you are always in public places when you are together with your girlfriend or boyfriend. It is far less likely that you will end up having sex if you are bowling with 30 people around. On the other hand, if you are parked in a car at night with soft music playing, you are obviously setting yourself up for failure.

Don't trust your date to maintain any type of moral standards. Don't even trust yourself. Self-control is simply not enough! Some couples have great intentions, but they also have sexual drives that can easily overcome their intentions. This is especially true if you're in the wrong place or with a person who is pressuring you to be physical. It's best to remove the need to even use self-control.

2. Wrong Person

Another reason that many young people give in sexually is simply because of whom they have chosen to date. If you decide to date someone who is already sexually active, then they will expect the same of you. Resisting premarital sex and saving yourself for your husband or wife can be extremely difficult. That's why you should only allow yourself to be interested in someone who has equally high standards in this area of their life. As I shared earlier, it's much easier to pull someone down morally than it is to pull them up.

If you are dating someone that has been sexually active in past relationships, then beware. You are much, much, much more likely to give in as well.

Once someone is used to having sexual activities in a relationship, it is very hard to stop. They may not pressure you for a little while, but before long, it will definitely become apparent.

It's natural to feel physically attracted to another person. It's natural to want to express that attraction. You can express it by saying sweet things, doing thoughtful things, or giving the other person gifts. If you try to express it physically however, then your physical desire will quickly escalate into sexual temptation that will be hard to resist.

Make it a prerequisite that whoever you decide to date in the future must have the same position on purity that you do. It is much more likely that you will both succeed if you see eye to eye on this issue. One young lady I met told me that everyone knows that she is saving herself for marriage. She said that this not only keeps her accountable to her friends, but it also lets potential would-be daters know where she stands before they even ask her out.

3. Wrong Mindset

How far can I go? How close can we get? Let's just do everything but have intercourse. These are perfect examples of what I call the wrong mindset.

The proper mindset should never be a matter of how close to sex you can get. It should be a matter of how far away from it you can get. As we will cover in the next chapter, once you start any form of physical intimacy, such as kissing, the pressure is going to increase to be more physical until the final sexual act has been committed. The only way to avoid that pressure is to choose not to get on that escalator at all.

Another example of the wrong mindset is the belief that "sex equals love." Let me make this clear: sex does not equal love.

Many young people have been deceived into thinking that having sex will bring them greater love, affection, closeness, commitment, and a more meaningful relationship. Instead, they often find emotional pain, rejection, and a lowered self-esteem. They find that their partner is only with them because of the sex or because they don't want to get hurt.

One young person admitted to me, "I slept with many people trying to find self-worth. And the more people I slept with, the less self-worth I had."

When a person devalues sex, they later feel that they have devalued themselves. The greatest thing you can ever give someone is you! You are unique and special! There is no one like you on the planet and when that gift is given out repeatedly, it is easy to begin to think less of yourself. Don't ever allow yourself to be fooled. Sex does not equal love, nor does it create love.

While some people wrongly think that sex will help them find love, others just use sex for its immediate gratification. They basically treat sex like a drug, and their partner like an object. Sex is an intimate act that involves every part of a person; physically, mentally, emotionally, and spiritually. In a sense, it is giving someone all of you. This is why sex was designed for marriage.

Sex is symbolic of that all-inclusive commitment that two people make to each other for life. Imagine how hard it will be for your spouse to accept that gift when you've already given it to other people. When sex is used outside of marriage, it damages the deepest parts of who we are.

A Few Dating Tips for Sexual Purity

- Avoid any time in a parked car with a date. Get out of the car quickly!
- Date with a group, or at the bare minimum, double date.
- Set a curfew, even if your parents do not.
- Never be alone with a person of the opposite sex, especially in your bedroom, dorm room, or parent's house.
- If a circumstance demands you to be in a room with a girlfriend or boyfriend, always leave the door open.
- Avoid alcohol and drugs. They eliminate most peoples' sexual boundaries.
- Avoid provocative dress. It's never a good idea to draw extra attention to your body.
- As a teenager, don't date someone who is two or more years older than you. In general they will expect more physical fulfillment than someone your own age.

If you want to come out a winner in this area, you have

to realize that the temptation to have premarital sex is very strong. When it comes to dating, wrong places, wrong people, and the wrong mindset cause wrong choices to be made. By setting up safeguards, you will protect yourself from potentially dangerous sexual situations.

SEX AND EFFECTS
WEEK 7

Group Review

Last week's lesson was on Foundation Breakers. Explain the connection between alcohol and drugs and the term "foundation breakers."

> "Flee from sexual immorality. All other sins a man commits are outside his body, but he who sins sexually sins against his own body." (1 Corinthians 6:18)

> "She caught him by his cloak and said, 'Come to bed with me!' But he left his cloak in her hand and ran out of the house." (Genesis 39:12)

1. What is the best way to avoid sexual immorality?

____

____

2. While all sin is bad, sexual sin is somehow a little different than other sins in that it is against our own ________. Something about this causes this sin to cause incredible emotional and psychological pain.

"Do you not know that your body is a temple of the Holy Spirit, who is in you, whom you have received from God? You are not your own; you were bought at a price. Therefore honor God with your body." (1 Corinthians 6:19-20)

3. A great question to ask yourself when determining how far is too far is, "Would I be honoring God with my body if I did that?" Remember, you are not your own, you are actually ________, and your body is the temple of the

__________________________.

Group Discussion

Do you think getting involved physically with someone could fool them into believing that they are more compatible than they really are?

____

"But among you there must not be even a hint of sexual immorality, or of any kind of impurity, or of greed, because these are improper for God's holy people." (Ephesians 5:3)

4. There should not even be a ________ of sexual immorality in our lives. Is being a technical virgin acceptable to God?

____

5. If you are ever being pressured to do something by someone of the opposite sex, even if it is kissing, should you break up with them? Explain.

____

____

____

6. Would it be more or less difficult for a Christian dating a non-Christian to remain pure until marriage? Why?

____

____

> "Put to death, therefore, whatever belongs to your earthly nature: sexual immorality, impurity, lust, evil desires and greed, which is idolatry." (Colossians 3:5)

7. What are some practical things that you can do to "put to death" these attributes of your sinful nature?

____

____

____

Group Discussion

What are some of the benefits for saving yourself for marriage?

____

____

____

> "For a man's ways are in full view of the Lord, and he examines all his paths." (Proverbs 5:21)

8. God sees everything. You are never hidden from God. He looks at our hearts, our thoughts and our actions. It is important to remember that just because nobody is around and you might be alone with that special someone, you are still "in full view of the_______."

Exercise

Why would the wrong person, wrong place, or the wrong mindset contribute to a teenager having sex before marriage. Take a moment to review each one.

STANDARDS FOR LOVING

CHAPTER 8

It's easy to see how drugs, alcohol, or premarital sex could damage our foundation but loving someone doesn't sound all that destructive. And since dating is all about falling in love, everyone seems to be dying to do it. But dating relationships aren't always beneficial and can even bring harm. I know that sounds weird, but let's take a closer look.

Puppy Love

I remember having my first girlfriend in the third grade. Her name was Kristen. I didn't know what it meant to have a girlfriend, but I had one. I even waved at her on the playground sometimes.

But in the fourth grade, that relationship came to an abrupt end. After recess, I was standing in line to go back to class. Another girl told one of her friends to ask me if I wanted to be her boyfriend. She was cute and funny, so I said yes. But before I did, I turned and told Kristen that I didn't like her anymore. I was oblivious to the potential embarrassment and sense of rejection that I might have caused her with my abrupt break up.

However, just two months later, Holly broke up with me in an equally abrupt manner for about the same shallow reason. Now this really hurt because I waved at her at least twice a week on the playground. Even though there was not much to lose, I still remember feeling rejected. Knowing that someone didn't like something about me was not enjoyable. But after years of extensive therapy, I was finally able to face myself. I might be exaggerating a little bit.

As I look back, it was a little ridiculous for me to have a girlfriend in the 3rd and 4th grade. I mean, what's the point? I, like the young ladies, was too young to fully understand what it meant. We were just doing what we observed others doing. I'm sure in retrospect of your own lives, you would agree that those early relationships were unnecessary, to say the least. The same point could be made for many of my junior high and high school relationships too.

As I think about those relationships, and how absolutely essential they seemed at the time, I just have to laugh. I would get so wrapped up in who my girlfriend was that I couldn't think about anything else. You know the drill: the letters, the check yes or no boxes, the drama, the dates, the emotional roller coaster, and the break ups.

Teenage Construction Zone

Like many people in grade school, I seemed to think that I needed to have someone I called my girlfriend. But as I look back, those relationships were not only unnecessary, but potentially dangerous. And the more I think about it, the more I realize that I probably would have been better off just having friends, instead of trying to label someone as my girlfriend.

The Purpose of Dating

In the 11th grade, my youth director told me something really deep. He told me that I was going to marry someone I dated.

Well of course, I thought. *That's obvious! You don't just marry a stranger. What a ridiculous thing to say.*

I missed the bigger point that he was trying to make. His point was that you shouldn't go out with a person that you would not marry. The qualities you desire in your eventual spouse should be the same qualities that you look for in a person that you date. Some people have lower standards for dating than they do for marriage, but in actuality, they should be one in the same. Never have a girlfriend or boyfriend just to have one, but make sure they are of marriage quality.

> Never go out with someone that you wouldn't marry.

If you can't find anyone that you would want to marry right now, don't give up. Be patient.

Don't go out just to go out. It's better to wait and find the right person than to rush things and get stuck with the wrong person. Some people think they can lower their standard for dating and still have a high standard for marriage. You can't.

Keep your standards high until you find a person that fulfills them. The people who meet your standards may not be in your classroom, your school, or even your town right now. But they are out there, and you have a whole lifetime to find them.

When Should I Date?

Young people frequently ask me when the right age to start dating is. There is not a single, specific age at which all people are mature enough to handle the pressures of dating. A good rule of thumb is that if a young person believes that having a particular boyfriend or girlfriend is absolutely necessary or the most important priority in their life, then they are not yet ready for a dating relationship.

Although I cannot give you the exact age of when you should date, I firmly believe that no one should start dating until they're at least sixteen years old. I'm not suggesting that everyone should date once they turn sixteen. What I'm saying is that sixteen is the earliest that anyone should think about having a boyfriend/girlfriend relationship.

By waiting until you're older, you are giving yourself more time to prepare for dating. The older you become, the more mature, emotionally stable, and sure of yourself you will be. Your chances of loving correctly are much higher if you've spent time building a strong foundation during these critical years, instead of spending them with a girlfriend or boyfriend. If you first spend a lot of time observing the relationships of others and viewing members of the opposite sex from the safe distance of friendship, you will know more about what you want and what to look for in the person that you date.

I know many of you think that you are mature enough to handle dating at much younger than sixteen. I thought the same thing. But in hindsight, I sure wish that I would have waited. I could have spent more time on things that were really important. I probably wasn't mature enough to date for all the right reasons until I was around twenty. And I'm not alone. Many people that have pushed so hard to date at a young age go on to regret their decisions.

One of the most successful teenagers I know right now wasn't allowed to have a girlfriend until he was sixteen. His parents told him that there was simply no need, and believe it or not he agreed!

Isaac was so busy with school, music, and football that he really didn't have time for a girlfriend. He knew that if he did have a girlfriend, the quality of the other areas of his life might suffer. His focus at this phase of his life was to mature into the best person that he could possibly be. Do you think he has any regrets? Let's see!

Isaac graduated high school with a 4.0 grade point average, learned to play the guitar, wrote his own music, became a four year letterman in football, set records, and was offered full scholarships by seven different universities. He doesn't have any emotional baggage with which he has to contend. He looks back at his decision to wait, and realizes that it was the right one. He has no regrets. Just lots of strength in his foundation and a whole lot of success.

Benefits of Waiting

One huge advantage to waiting to date is that the longer you wait to date, the less likely you are to have premarital sex. As we discussed in the last chapter, sex outside of marriage is a huge danger that should be avoided at all costs. In his book *The Myth of Safe Sex,* John Ankerberg shares the link between dating young and sex. This study relates the age girls began to date to the likelihood of having sex before marriage:

- Of those who started dating at twelve, 90% had sex before marriage.
- Of those who started dating at thirteen, 58% had sex before marriage.
- Of those who started dating at fourteen, 50% had sex before marriage.
- Of those who started dating at fifteen, 40% had sex before marriage.
- Of those who started dating at sixteen, 19% had sex before marriage.
- Of those who started dating at seventeen, 15% had sex before marriage.[23]

Teenage Construction Zone

Many people do more damage than good to their foundation by getting into relationships too early. You should never feel that you have to be dating someone or that you are required to be in a relationship. This is a sad misconception. Television shows and popular culture seem to push this idea onto young people. But just because something is popular does not mean that it's good for you. There is a better way.

You don't have to date! One of the greatest advantages of waiting is the ability to enjoy being around friends. It is possible to have life-enriching friendships with people of the opposite sex without having to have a romantic relationship. You will be far better off if you just have girl or boy friends, not girlfriends or boyfriends.

Not dating allows you just to be you. You don't have to be constantly consumed with what that other person thinks of you or if they're thinking of you. You're free; free to pursue your dreams, goals, life, and fun with your friends. I want to challenge you to go against the flow on this issue. So many young people spend these precious years of their life pursuing romance, just to find that they regret it in the future.

Completely Captivated

When people are not emotionally secure in who they are as a person, they can become totally and completely consumed by thoughts of someone else. They neglect everyone and everything around them just to try to please this one person. Grades and performance in extracurricular activities can easily begin to plummet. Their friends, parents, and siblings all but vanish to the overwhelming infatuation with their new "love." Then, when the almost inevitable break up happens, they realize they sacrificed so much for nothing.

The longer you date, the harder it is to imagine life without that person. I shared with you earlier that I don't drink alcohol, but in college, I made a big mistake. I dated someone for two years who did. She was constantly getting drunk. But I was in love. I tried to ignore the problem and hoped that she would change one day.

As a side note, you should never date someone with the hope of changing them into the person you want them to be. Although there are exceptions, people are who they are. Who they are now is usually a good indicator of who they will be in the future.

> *You should never date someone with the hope of changing them into the person you want them to be.*

To make a long story short, my relationship with this girl didn't last. She, of course, didn't change. In fact, her drinking problem got even worse, which led us to breaking up. Looking back now, I can't believe I even agreed to date her. I can't believe I gave her two years of my life. People around me tried to warn me, but I was blinded by my feelings of love. I strived to keep my standards so high in my own life, yet I unwittingly jeopardized my future by dating the wrong person.

> *Your future spouse is like a diamond. They may be rare, but they are worth the wait.*

Just as I encouraged you to raise and keep your moral standards high, I also want you to know that it's just as important to make sure that your boyfriend or girlfriend has the same moral standards that you do. One of the quickest ways for teens to get off track during their foundational years is to date the wrong person.

Quality, Not Quantity

I had a friend in high school that always made it a point to tell me how many girls he was dating at one time. It was a source of pride with him to brag about it. I wasn't impressed because I knew him, and I knew the type of girls that he dated. They may have been attractive, but they weren't the kind of people that you would want to have a relationship with.

Dating is serious. When it's time to date, don't just date anyone or everyone, but keep your standards high. It might mean that you have to be more selective with whom you will date. But that's ok. Your future spouse is like a diamond. They may be rare, but they are worth the wait. And they are out there. You won't have to wait forever.

Application and References Please

When it is finally time to start the process of selecting a girlfriend or boyfriend, be extremely careful. Others may think of it as not a big deal, but believe me, it's a huge deal! You are letting someone into your life that has the potential to make a big impact on your foundation.

Choosing a boyfriend or girlfriend should be approached like a company hiring an employee. When employers hire someone for a position in their company, they will take applications, do interviews, get background checks, and research a person as much as they possibly can. Why? Because the future of that company is in that person's hands!

How much more important is the person that will be playing such a key role in your life. You should not place the title "girlfriend" or "boyfriend" on anyone without a lot of research. Now, I'm not suggesting résumés, criminal background checks or being a creepy stalker, but I am suggesting that you find out all that you can about a person before you get too close.

You will learn a lot just by watching them around other people. Ask them important questions about religion, their other relationships, purity issues, morals, etc. You can also get a good idea of who they are by who their friends are.

Some might think I am going a little overboard here but remember what is at stake. This is your life, your future! When you date someone, you are looking to see if they qualify to be your spouse for the rest of your life and the

Dating is the process of choosing someone to build your life with.

parent of your eventual children. There is a lot on the line here. Dating is not just a fun little game. It is the process of choosing someone to build your life with.

Also, be aware that even if someone talks the talk, you need to make sure that they walk the walk. They might say all the right things but are they living it? Words are cheap and easily spoken. People know what you want to hear, but that's where careful observation and time come into play. Before you move a relationship to the next level, make sure that the person you're interested in is really who you think they are.

Finally, remember to choose someone for the right reasons. A friend once told me that most people enter into a relationship with someone with their 95/5 backwards. Ninety-five percent of what makes us choose someone should be qualities like their character, morals, honesty, reputation, purity, integrity, and trustworthiness. What they look like should only influence 5% of our decision.

Instead, we usually choose someone based 95% on appearance and only 5% on what really matters. While it's not at all wrong to date or marry someone who is pleasing to your eyes, just remember that charm and beauty can be very deceptive. Don't just look skin deep. Look at who that person really is on the inside.

Escalation

The longer you date someone, the easier it is to become physically intimate with that person. I call it the escalation effect.

An elementary example of the escalation effect might go something like this. At first a young man might yawn, stretch, and put his arm around a young lady at the movies. Before long, as they get more and more comfortable with each other, they begin to hold hands, and the escalation continues.

> *The longer you date someone, the easier it becomes to be physically intimate.*

In the weeks to come, maybe she'll give him a small kiss on the cheek. Weeks later, maybe the small kiss has turned into much longer, more drawn out kisses. After couples reach this point, they usually try to find more places to be alone together. They will desire more and more physical touch and so the escalation continues.

There is no need to go on any further with the progression, you get the point. Sometimes teenagers say that they have made the admirable choice to wait until they are married to have sex. They mean well, but then they start dating. They find themselves progressing ever closer to that moment by allowing themselves to become more and more physical in their display of affection. It's not enough just to make a commitment to save yourself for marriage.

Don't get me wrong, I firmly believe that young people should make the commitment to wait to have sex. However, you also have to commit to stopping the progression of intimacy that leads to that act. As Dr. James Dobson says in *Life on the Edge*, "The decision not to have sexual intercourse should be made long before the opportunity presents itself. Steps can then be taken to slow the natural progression before it gets started."[24]

In other words, the act of sex is not just one bad decision, but the result of many smaller bad decisions.

Let me give you an old parable about cooking a frog. If you boil hot water and then drop a frog into it, he will feel the extreme difference in temperature and jump right out. If you put the frog in room temperature water, and then start slowly heating the water up, he won't feel the gradual change. He'll just sit there until he dies.

> The act of sex is not just one bad decision, but the result of many smaller bad decisions.

This is similar to what happens to many teenagers. They get desensitized to the escalation because it happens slowly over time. The temperature keeps rising and the physical escalation continues until it's too late. So what does it look like to successfully avoid the escalation process?

While in college at the University of Arkansas, I attended a church that had a large collegiate ministry. I had the utmost respect for their student minister, because I had seen the way that he lived. We were all surprised to discover one day that our student leader was dating someone. He had integrity in every area of his life and dating proved to be no different.

I noticed after a few months that he and his girlfriend never seemed to touch. I mean not at all. They didn't even hold hands.

Curiosity got the best of me, so I asked him why they never showed any physical affection. He said the reason was because they cared about each other so much.

He confided that he had messed up sexually as a teen, and at this point in his life, he totally understood the sexual temptation that dating can cause. In order to prevent anything like that from happening again, his girlfriend and he restricted virtually all physical contact. At their wedding one year later, they kissed for the very first time!

I know the story sounds too good to be true, but it isn't. These two people who loved each other dearly had committed themselves to keeping their relationship pure. They determined that the best way was to not even begin the escalation process. Wow! What an example of choosing to do the right thing no matter what your emotions are telling you.

You must realize that physical escalation is automatic. Unless you are intentional about stopping physical escalation before it gets too far, then you are almost guaranteed to eventually have sex with your girlfriend or boyfriend. It is important to determine where you stand before you ever find yourself in this type of situation.

Draw your moral lines, and stick to them. Be up front with all potential dates about your moral convictions. If they object, disagree, or just don't understand, then keep on looking. You're better off not wasting any time dating them.

Where to Draw the Line

I know what some of you are wondering just how far is too far. That's a fair question. It's a question that every person should answer before they are in a situation where they have to make a decision. If you wait until then, odds are you won't be thinking clearly enough to make the right decision.

After meeting thousands of people every year, looking back at my life, researching, and thinking a lot about what I will soon be telling my very own daughters, here is my answer. Now, make sure you're sitting down because what you are about to read goes against everything you've been taught by TV, song lyrics, and many of your friends. Are you ready? Are you sure? Here it goes.

To start, let me remind you that your goal is not to see how far you can go without going all the way. With that said, the safest and most ideal line to draw when it comes to physical contact is nothing beyond holding hands.

If you truly believe that both of you can restrain yourself, you are at least an older teenager, and in a very committed relationship, then kissing could be permitted, but definitely not required. I'm not talking about a make out session here. I would suggest nothing more than an occasional quick kiss, nothing longer than a couple of seconds. But beware; even kissing can escalate out of control as well.

Couples should always incorporate the vertical rule as well. No matter where you are, never be lying down together. It is just asking for trouble. Another great rule of thumb to go by when deciding how far is too far, is to do nothing with a boyfriend/girlfriend that you could not do in front of your parents, grandparents, your siblings, or even your pastor.

Well, how'd it go? Don't throw the book away or stop reading yet. I am well aware that the above paragraph is a bit hard to swallow. I know many of you might think that these guidelines are way too strict or even absurd, but anything more than this has too great of a chance to cause you to progress rapidly toward a sexual relationship and all the consequences that it brings. I promise that you will never look back and regret setting up such strong standards in this area of your life.

Remember, your foundation is underway. Your entire life is going to depend on it very soon. These guidelines that I have suggested are made with your whole life in mind. Yes, they are a bit painful now, but they are saving you from far greater pain later. These guidelines might appear ridiculously impossible to stick to, but they're not. If you are dating the right person at the right places, and with the right mindset, your odds of success will be high.

So, where are you going to draw the line? What will your standards be? Developing your own personal standards for loving is a critical part of your foundation. As you think about this, remember that what is best is usually not what is popular, and it's not always what you feel is right.

How to Break Up 101

One of the most important things to learn before starting any relationship is how to end a relationship. I know that sounds mean and heartless at first, but you will have to break up with someone, possibly many people in your life. Almost every dating relationship you have will eventually end in a break up. You should know how to get out of a relationship in a way that doesn't crush the other person.

Personally, I was horrible at breaking up. I never could do it. Instead of breaking up with a girl when I knew we weren't right for each other, I would just keep on going out until finally they dumped me. I hated confrontation, and I didn't want to deal with any drama that might occur.

Looking back, I wish someone would have given me a few suggestions in the area of breaking up. I've tried to provide you with a list of do's and don'ts so that you can face this situation with a little more preparation.

A Few Don'ts to Remember:

- Don't let the relationship continue for longer than it should.
- Don't try to hurt them or humiliate them.
- Don't tell them everything that you don't like about them.
- Don't spread gossip about them.
- Don't keep calling, texting, or seeing them. Put some space in between you. This helps each of you heal and

get focused on moving on.

- Don't find someone else right away. That makes the last relationship seem meaningless and unimportant to the person you just broke up with. That hurts. Plus, you need time between relationships to clear your mind of emotions so that you can make healthy, rational decisions about your future and future relationships.

A Few Do's to Remember:

- Do break up with them privately (not yelling at them down the school hallway).
- Do be clear that you want to break up. Don't try to slip it by them or just hope they will figure it out.
- Do stay broken up for at least one or two months. This lets emotions die down and helps you to think more clearly.
- Do break up with them like you would want someone to break up with you. No one wants to get broken up with so treat them with respect and dignity.

Breaking up is never easy and usually hurts, but it is a necessary quality to acquire. By learning the right way to break up with someone, you do yourself and all future boyfriends/girlfriends a huge favor. You allow for the possibility of still being friends with the person you just broke up with. Breaking up is a part of life, but try to make it as painless as possible for the both of you.

Getting Broken Up With

Being on the receiving end of a break up is probably a little more painful than being the one doing the breaking up. So what should you do in this situation?

A Few Don'ts to Remember:

- Don't lash out and try to hurt them. Yes, you are hurt, but saying bad things about the person will not help the matter.
- Don't keep calling, texting or seeing them. They have made the point that they want to be apart so allow them to do so. This helps each of you to think clearer, and protects your dignity.
- Don't think it is the end of the world. I guarantee you will meet someone that is a better fit for you.
- Don't isolate yourself. Being alone after a break up only leads to being consumed with the issue.
- Don't go right into another relationship. You need some time to truly get over this.

A Few Do's to Remember:

- Do honor their request for a break up. Don't try to fight it.
- Do allow a brief time for reflection. It's good to figure out what went wrong in a relationship so that you can prevent it in your future relationships. Make sure that it's only for a day or two though. You need to learn

and move on.

- Do stay busy. Hang out with friends, watch a movie, spend time with your family. This keeps your mind from dwelling on the issue.

Look at break ups as a positive thing. I know it sounds ridiculous, and it's the last thing you want to hear when you've just been broken up with. But break ups allow you to get away from someone who wasn't right for you and do some quality soul searching.

Sometimes you can't see any problems in a relationship until you are out of it for a while. So use the experience as a guide to help you pick someone that is more suited for you in the future. Break ups allow you the chance to get on with life and get back to finding the person you are truly supposed to be with.

STANDARDS FOR LOVING
WEEK 8

Group Review

Why would the wrong person, wrong place, or the wrong mindset contribute to a teenager having sex before marriage? Take a moment to discuss each one.

1. Where do most peoples' standards for loving come from?

____

____

"…treat younger men as brothers…and younger women as sisters, with absolute purity." (1 Timothy 5:1-2)

2. Do you think of your peers as brothers and sisters? Of course you would not look at a brother or sister lustfully, but the Bible says that we should treat everyone of the opposite sex in that manner. Remember, even if you have a boyfriend or girlfriend, they are not yours. They are God's property.

Group Discussion

"Therefore, I urge you, brothers, in view of God's mercy, to offer your bodies as living sacrifices, holy and pleasing to God—this is your spiritual act of worship." (Romans 12:1)

A sacrifice to God in the Old Testament was something that was totally consumed by fire. Every part of it was given to the Lord. Why does Paul say here that we are to be living sacrifices? How could this verse apply to setting your standards for loving?

____

____

____

"Each of you should learn to control his own body in a way that is holy and honorable, not in passionate lust like the heathen, who do not know God; and that in this matter no one should wrong his brother or take advantage of him. The Lord will punish men for all such sins, as we have already told you and warned you. For God did not call us to be impure, but to live a holy life. Therefore, he who rejects this instruction does not reject man but God, who gives you his Holy Spirit." (1 Thessalonians 4:4-8)

3. In order to be obedient to God, you should learn to ___________ your body, and not let it control you. Even if the people you're around don't expect you to live a pure life, it doesn't matter. God, your creator has called you to be pure and holy!

4. If you decide to reject this teaching, then who, according to this passage, are you rejecting? __________

> "Watch and pray so that you will not fall into temptation. The spirit is willing, but the body is weak." (Mathew 26:41)

5. What does Jesus say to do to avoid falling into temptation?

____

Spend a moment in prayer today on this topic. Pray that you will not give in to temptation and will set the standards for love that Jesus himself would approve of.

> "Do not be yoked together with unbelievers. For what do righteousness and wickedness have in common? Or what fellowship can light have with darkness? ... What does a believer have in common with an unbeliever?" (2 Corinthians 6:14-15)

6. We looked at this verse earlier and related it to our friendships, but how does this verse relate specifically to a potential girlfriend/boyfriend?

____

____

Group Discussion

Do you believe it is easier for you to influence a non-Christian boyfriend/girlfriend or for them to influence you? Why?

____

____

____

"A wife of noble character is her husband's crown,
but a disgraceful wife is like decay in his bones."
(Proverbs 12:4)

"Charm is deceptive, and beauty is fleeting; but a
woman who fears the Lord is to be praised."
(Proverbs 31:30)

7. Is it easy to desire someone for the wrong reasons? God challenges us to look beyond the exterior of a person, and find out who they really are on the inside.

____

____

Exercise

Reread the escalation portion of this chapter. Where are you going to draw the line? When you have set these boundaries, find an accountability partner and let them know about them. Make a commitment to check up on each others' physical relationships when they become a temptation.

THE DECEPTION OF SUICIDE

CHAPTER 9

I went to speak at a school in Wisconsin a few years back. The principal was glad to see me, but you could tell there was a lot of concern in her eyes. She said that she had lost six young people to suicide in the current semester alone.

What a horrible tragedy! These students had ended their life when it was just getting started. They would never go on to experience the joys of graduation, college, careers, travelling, marriage, children, or grandchildren. They had made a horrible choice, and there was no return.

There are no words to describe how bad of a decision these young people had made. Obviously, they had deceived themselves into thinking that they were not important. They were not thinking of their future but were feeling overwhelmed by a temporary problem.

The Journey of Life

Life is a journey, and in any long journey, you will have to overcome a variety of terrains. Sometimes your journey might take you to the top of a mountain peak. Sometimes, you might be relaxing and taking it easy on a beach.

Other times you will find yourself down in a valley. It's in that moment that so many people give up on life. They convince themselves that life is horrible, and it will never get any better.

Please remember that if you find yourself down in a valley of despair, see the problem through, keep moving, and before long you will come out the other side. It would be nice if nothing bad ever happened to us, but that just is not possible. Always realize that the journey keeps going, and that you will not always be in this valley. It might last a day, a week, or months, but you can and will make it through.

It's the tough times in life that often develop a person's character the most. What we perceive to be storms should really be looked at as schooling. When you're going through a hard time, you shouldn't just ask "why," but "what." What about this situation is making you stronger or better? Often times, there's more to be learned in the valleys of your life than on the mountain tops.

Suicide should never be considered a valid option for you, no matter what you are going through. Suicide is a permanent solution to a temporary problem! Whatever problems you are facing now, or will face in the future, will not last forever. No matter how hopeless you might feel at the moment, I promise that there is a better solution to the problem. Never quit. Never give up. See the problem through, and you will be glad you did.

Break Up Blues

Believe it or not, many teenagers tell me that break ups are something that have caused them to think irrationally about life and death.

I remember falling "in love" with a young lady as I was going through school. I knew beyond a shadow of a doubt that this was the girl for me. She was beautiful, nice, fun, and someone that I thought I would like to be around forever.

We were together all the way through high school. I even bought her a promise ring before I went off to college, letting her know that when the time was right, we would get married. I went off to the University of Arkansas while she was still in high school some four and a half hours away.

To make a long story short, I had been at college for about a semester when she let me know that she wanted to see other people. I couldn't believe it. I mean, this was the girl that I had trusted with my life. I just knew that we would always be together. For years we both believed that to be true.

But all of the sudden, in a matter of seconds, it was all over. I was panicked, mad, sad, angry, and confused. It just didn't make sense to me. It seemed like my entire world had just come crashing down!

But life got back to normal a lot quicker than I ever thought it would. Yes, I was down in the dumps and depressed for a little while, but in a matter of weeks, I was back on my feet again. I stayed active, surrounded myself with good friends and family, and made a point not to dwell on thoughts of her or the break up.

Since then I have been blessed with an amazing wife that is everything I could have asked for. She's beautiful both inside and out. She is my best friend, someone that brings joy to me like no one else in the world possibly could. She is the person that I can truly trust with my life and my children. I have two precious daughters, Allie and Tapanga, who mean the world to me. I get to travel around the globe and encourage thousands of great young people just like you. But none of that would have come to pass if I had ended my life during college.

It's important to realize that break ups happen to everybody. Ninety-eight percent of all relationships end in a break up.[25] That fact may not seem all that consoling, but it does help to know that virtually every person has been in those shoes before, including me. I made it through, and you will too.

In fact, break ups can even end up being a positive event. Just think, if my girlfriend hadn't dumped me, I wouldn't have the amazing wife that I have now. Who knows how my life would be.

Younique

Besides break ups, many young people commit suicide because they feel like they are worthless. Many teenagers feel less important because they compare themselves to others and find that they are lacking some quality that the other person has. Of course, you will never find your importance this way, because you're not supposed to be like everyone else!

You're not suppose to be like everyone else! You're unique.

Take Nick Vujicic, for example. Nick was born without arms or legs. Just try to imagine what his life must have been like as a child, as a teenager, and now as an adult. No amount of imagination could ever portray an accurate picture of the struggles that he has faced. People might say that Nick has every right to believe that he is worthless. What could he possibly do with his life? So, what does Nick actually do with his life?

Nick is a powerful motivational speaker that travels around the world specializing on the topic of joy! Some of his more famous speeches are titled "No Arms, No Legs, No Worries," and "How I Went from No Legs to No Limits." Imagine that; severely handicapped and speaking on joy.

You see, Nick understands that life isn't about fitting in. It's not about comparing yourself to others. Life is about being the best you possibly can! Nick's difference doesn't make him worthless. It makes him great!

Many teenagers make the mistake of comparing themselves to others in order to find significance. Oftentimes they end up feeling more insignificant than ever. Just think if Nick would have used this tactic to find his significance and how easy it would have been for him to feel depressed.

Comparing yourself to others is always going to be an unfair comparison. Odds are that you will compare their obvious strengths to your weaknesses. You might wish you had someone's good looks, but they might wish they had your intellect. You have to realize that each person has characteristics and talents that are specific to them.

During high school and middle school, it's tempting to fit everyone into certain stereotypes. Sometimes you might think that if you're not the star football player, captain of the cheerleaders, or the most attractive person in school, you're somehow less important. But don't be fooled.

I have seen those who were considered lost causes turn into successful lawyers. I have seen the "un-datable" turn into the best husband and father that a woman could ever ask for. Everyone has the seeds of greatness within them, but often times the seeds take longer to discover and develop than we'd like.

You have a lot of living left to do. Odds are that whatever gets you down now will pass away sooner than you think. Your journey is just beginning! There are a million possibilities out there for you.

So who is important? Is it the movie star? The professional athlete? The top musical artist? The millionaire?

The answer is all of the above. Importance is more than popularity, riches, and fame. Every single human on the planet is important. The people that I listed above are not important because of what they do. They are important because they are! Likewise, you are important not because of what you do, but because you are.

> *You are important because you are you, not because of what you do.*

There is no one else on this planet like you. There has never been before, nor will there be after. In the entire universe and all of time there is only one of you. You are unique. You are needed to fulfill a role that only you can fulfill. No matter how you may feel at the moment, you are extremely important!

Get Help!

If you ever find yourself having suicidal thoughts, it's very important to talk to someone about it. People who are depressed usually aren't thinking clearly. Sometimes it's hard to see out of the dark cloud that you're in. Depressed people only think of the problem and nothing else. But for someone on the outside of the problem looking in, it can be much easier.

It is critical to ask qualified people for help. These might be your grandparents, aunts or uncles, siblings, your pastor, a teacher, a coach, or your school counselor.

I know many young people may not want to hear this, but your parents can be a valuable aid in understanding and helping. Whatever you are going through, they have probably experienced or know others who have.

Whoever it is that you decide to trust, don't fight the battle by yourself. Find someone to help you.

THE DECEPTION OF SUICIDE

WEEK 9

Group Review

Last week's chapter was about setting standards for the way you love. Give some good ideas and some bad ideas when it comes to breaking up. Why is it important to know how to break up, and how to deal with getting broken up with?

Group Discussion

Why do you think teenagers become completely consumed by a few specific problems?

"The Lord is a refuge for the oppressed, a stronghold in times of trouble." (Psalm 9:9)

"Find rest, O my soul, in God alone; my hope comes from him. He alone is my rock and my salvation; he is my fortress, I will not be shaken. My salvation and my honor depend on God; he is my mighty rock, my refuge." (Psalm 62:5-7)

"God is our refuge and strength, an ever-present help in trouble." (Psalm 46:1)

1. From the verses above, list some things that God is called.

____

____

> "For our light and momentary troubles are achieving for us an eternal glory that far outweighs them all. So we fix our eyes not on what is seen, but on what is unseen. For what is seen is temporary, but what is unseen is eternal."
> (2 Corinthians 4:17-18)

2. Everyone goes through hard times. The early Christians were tortured and tormented, yet they kept their eyes on Jesus. No matter what problems you face you'll get through them a lot easier and faster when you focus on God and not the problem. What are some things you can do when times are bad to keep your eyes on God?

____

____

____

> "I know what it is to be in need, and I know what it is to have plenty. I have learned the secret of being content in any and every situation, whether well fed or hungry, whether living in plenty or in want. I can do everything through him who gives me strength."
> (Philippians 4:12-13)

3. When people rely only on themselves to make it through problems, they often fall short. Who does the passage above say to rely on for strength?

____

"I always pray with joy…being confident of this, that he who began a good work in you will carry it on to completion until the day of Christ Jesus." (Philippians 1:4b-6)

4. Difficult times will come into your life, but Christ is more than able to get you through them. You can be "______________ of this."

"Do not be anxious about anything, but in everything, by prayer and petition, with thanksgiving, present your requests to God. And the peace of God, which transcends all understanding, will guard your hearts and your minds in Christ Jesus." (Philippians 4:6-7)

5. We make our problems even bigger when we dwell on them. Instead, as Christians, what should we do according to the verse above?

____

____

6. What does it say will happen when we do that?

____

____

"For you created my inmost being; you knit me together in my mother's womb. I praise you because I am fearfully and wonderfully made; your works are wonderful, I know that full well. My frame was not hidden from you when I was made in the secret place. When I was woven together in the depths of the earth, your eyes saw my unformed body. All the days ordained for me

were written in your book before one of them
came to be." (Psalm 139:13-16)

7. God has a plan and purpose for your life. Do you sometimes forget that you were wonderfully made? You are so special that he even sent Jesus to die for all of your sins. That way you can confess your sins to him, believe in Jesus, and be saved. ________ designed you that way!

"If we confess or sins, he is faithful and just and
will forgive us our sins and purify us from all
unrighteousness." (1 John 1:9)

8. Some people allow past sins to get them extremely depressed. What does this verse say that God does when we confess our sins?

____

____

Group Discussion

Some people think that they have done things that God would never forgive. Is there any truth behind this? What advice would you give to someone your own age who is struggling to forgive themselves for something they've done in the past?

____

____

9. If you ever have a friend that struggles with suicidal feelings, what are some things that you could do or say to help?

____

____

____

Exercise

Even if you're not facing any troubles at the moment, come up with a plan this week of what to do and who to talk to if you ever begin feeling depressed and discouraged. Write it down and keep it somewhere safe for when trouble strikes.

HEALTH AND FITNESS

CHAPTER 10

What do you think of when you hear *health and fitness*? Something negative, like a PE coach making you run or a health teacher telling you not to drink sodas (or pop, for you northerners)?

My mind immediately goes back to a health class that I had to take in the ninth grade. It was so boring, except when they showed us the gross pictures of what certain diseases or drugs do to people. Then it was just scary.

Later, I realized that the health and fitness classes were a lot more important than I originally had thought. Choices regarding exercise and nutrition are very important parts of your foundation because it will have a great impact on how well you are able to enjoy life.

I'm not looking at this subject merely from a superficial viewpoint. Health and fitness doesn't mean looking like an underwear model with perfect curves or ripped muscles.

You've probably put too much of that type of pressure on yourself already without me adding more. I don't think you should look a certain way at all.

> 63% of high schoolers are no longer physically active.

Exercise and good nutrition are more important than just improving your appearance. They improve your body's overall performance. Your heart, lungs, muscles, bones, ligaments, tendons, blood composition, and even how long you will live are all affected by your exercise and nutrition habits, or lack thereof.

Don't skip the chapter just because you're not overweight. Don't think only morbidly large people need to exercise and eat right. Every teenager is supposed to get at least one hour of exercise a day, and every teenager should make their health a priority. You probably get at least an hour of TV or time on the computer each day.

Did you know that 63% of high school students are no longer physically active?[25] This, along with unhealthy eating habits, has caused a severe increase in overweight and obese teenagers. The majority of these teens will carry those habits on into their adulthood where they will continue to reap the full consequences of their choices.

Many of these people will suffer problems with their heart, lungs, and joints. A large number will develop type 2 diabetes. Some will even die prematurely. In most cases, all this could have been prevented by making different choices during their teenage years.

The point of this chapter is to take a closer look at how the health habits you are forming now will affect you throughout the rest of your life. How you treat your body now determines how it is going to treat you later, so treat it right!

> *How you treat your body now determines how it is going to treat you later.*

Exercise

Before we go any further, let's look at why you should exercise in the first place. The benefits of exercise that I have found in my research and personal experience include:

- Reduced risk of developing and/or dying from heart disease[26]
- Reduced blood pressure[27]
- Reduced cholesterol[28]
- Reduced risk of certain cancers[29]
- Reduced risk of developing diabetes[30]
- Reduced amount of body fat[31]
- Reduced risk of premature death[32]
- Added strength in muscles, bones, and joints[33]
- Help in combating various chronic diseases[34]
- Better sleep[35]

- Improved attitude[36]
- Improved intellect[37]
- Stress relief[38]
- And don't forget, it can also be fun!

Be Creative

Exercise isn't just for athletes. Exercise is for everyone. There are literally thousands of different ways to do it. Just because you don't like running doesn't mean there is no hope for you. If you just think of exercise as work, you're less likely to make it a habit. Find a kind of exercise that you actually enjoy. Believe it or not, that does exist.

Besides running, you could ride a bike, walk, jog, skateboard, skate, hike, canoe, ski, lift weights, try an exercise video, do aerobics, gymnastics, yoga, or martial arts, dance, swim, or play Frisbee golf. You could join school sports or a gym class. It's a little easier to get your exercise in when it's just a part of your daily school routine.

If you can't exercise at school, find time to do it at home. Try to find a friend to exercise with. You can hold each other accountable and have fun hanging out at the same time. The key is to find something you enjoy and stick to it.

Be Consistent

Today, we expect immediate results for what we want. If I need an answer to a question, I just ask Google. If I want a new song, I can download it in seconds. Reaping the benefits of exercise is not like that.

Don't give up after one or two tries. You can't just expect to go for a jog one day and end up healthy, muscular, and full of energy the next. You have to be consistent.

Exercising one day a week isn't going to do much. But if you start routinely exercising 3-5 days a week, then your body is going to start changing. The more consistently you exercise, the easier it will become. However, be cautious not to over exercise. Your body does need a couple days off every week.

Be Disciplined

If you consistently exercise but are not involved in a team sport, then you are probably even more disciplined than your school's star athlete. Why?

Don't rely on your parents to tell you to stay active!

Your school's star athlete has a coach that helps drive them and push them. You may have to be your own coach. But that's good. For the vast majority of your life, no one is going to coach you. If you learn self-discipline with exercise, then you will have added a strong brick to your foundation.

Don't rely on your parents to tell you when or what to do to stay active either. Make it a point to take it personal. I mean, it is *your* body.

You will have to be intentional about exercising. It's easy

to let other, less important things crowd out your day. Being fit doesn't just happen on its own.

You might need to wake up earlier or sacrifice some TV or computer time. Be disciplined. Start some kind of routine. After a few weeks, it will turn into a habit. You'll get so used to it that you will feel weird if you don't exercise.

Nutrition

> *Knowledge is the greatest tool for maintaining your health.*

Exercising is just one aspect to what your body needs. The other is nutrition.

Your body is made up of the stuff you put in it. From your skin down to your bones, what goes into your mouth determines the health of almost every part of your body. Being smart about nutrition means that you are careful with what you put in your mouth.

Your busy schedule may lead you to skip breakfast, buy lunch from vending machines, and grab whatever is in the refrigerator for dinner when you get home. These types of eating habits will not help you cope with the demand that is being placed on your body physically, mentally, or emotionally.

Healthy behaviors, like nutritious eating and regular physical activity, can help you meet the challenges of your life. Healthy eating may help you feel energized, learn better, and stay alert in class.

Not a Diet, a Way of Life

Some teens use unhealthy tactics to help them lose weight, including cutting out whole groups of foods (like grain products), skipping meals, and not eating altogether. This is a big mistake at anytime in your life but especially during your foundational years. These methods can leave out important foods you need to grow and develop. Unhealthy dieting can even put you at greater risk for emotional problems.[39] And believe it or not, unhealthy dieting can actually cause you to gain weight and tempt you to binge eat or overeat.[40] So if dieting isn't the answer, then what is? Knowledge, and then self-discipline.

Knowledge is the greatest tool for maintaining your health. I've met so many people who thought they were eating healthy until they put a little time into studying what eating healthy actually means. Take time to learn about nutrition. You can find out anything in a matter of seconds on the internet. This is the information age.

It is sad that most schools only require one nutrition class to graduate high school. There are some subjects that you may use once a month if you're lucky, but you eat every day, multiple times a day. Yet, many people choose to never learn about good nutrition. Instead, they just go with the flow. They eat what everyone else is eating, value size their meals, and still expect to have a healthy body. That's not the way it works.

Teenage Construction Zone

Little changes in your diet actually add up to make big changes over time. Don't get into too big of a rush. Just be consistent, and you'll get to where you want to be. Here are a few tips to get you going:

Start with simple things, like learning more about the Dietary Guidelines for America and the recommended daily amounts of nutrients that you should be getting. These standards take the guess work out of eating healthy.

Learn how to understand food labels. Almost every food item you buy has a label on it that tells you what's in it. It's there for your own good.

Just because it's on your plate doesn't mean you have to eat it. You probably have more food in front of you than you really need. Smaller portions can be a great way to maintain a healthy weight.

Try to make smarter food choices at fast food restaurants. Years ago, if you were eating fast food, it was just a given that it was going to be high in fat. Today, virtually every fast food restaurant has healthy alternatives. Instead of a cheeseburger, fries, and a coke, get a grilled chicken sandwich, fruit, and low fat milk. Boom! You have a drastically lowered your calories, fat, carbohydrates, and even add some much needed vitamins and minerals.

Little things, like using mustard or ketchup on your sandwich instead of mayonnaise can also make a big difference. This reduces up to 25 grams of fat from your meal. Avoid any fried foods. Eating greasy foods is never a good way to stay healthy.

Watch what you drink. Sodas are a bad choice because they are loaded in sugar and void of nutrition. Choose better drinks like water, low fat milk, or juice. (Drink smaller amounts of juice though. They do have good nutrients in them, but they are also usually pretty high in sugar.)

Take your own lunch to school as often as you can so you know exactly what you are eating. Try to include fruits and vegetables, low fat milk and cheese, lean meats, chicken, beans, fish, and whole grains for good carbohydrates. For example, use whole-grain bread to make a turkey sandwich. Throw in some baked chips and a piece of fruit and you're all set.

Eat slower. If you can, talk with your friends or family in between bites. Ask them questions. Be social. This added time gives your brain more time to tell your stomach that it's full. Even slowing down to drink most of your drink before you eat can help you feel more satisfied without having eaten so much food.

Let your parents know that you are trying to have a healthier, low fat diet. Politely ask them to be aware of that when they are grocery shopping or volunteer to go with them to the store. With all the research that you've done, you may know more than your parents about nutrition. If nobody in your home cooks dinner or breakfast very often, try cooking for yourself or the rest of your family. Just because it's healthy doesn't mean that you have to spend a lot of time on it or be a world class chef.

Eat breakfast, lunch, and supper. Do your best not to skip a meal. Don't expect to be at 100% of your learning capacity at school if you didn't eat breakfast. By not eating, you are starving your body of many nutrients that you desperately need during the day. If you skipped breakfast, your mood will be affected, your attention span will be shorter, you'll feel tired, and your brain won't be working fully. Skipping meals also makes you eat even more food later.

Snack smart. Don't fool yourself, snacks add up. They can be a major factor in your general health. A lot of snacks are nothing but flour and sugar. Try to incorporate snacks that are healthier such as fruit, baked chips, low-fat popcorn, whole grain crackers, low fat string cheese, nuts, low fat yogurts, certain granola bars, beef jerky, etc.

Get Control

> *While knowledge is the greatest tool, self-discipline is second.*

While knowledge is the greatest tool to build your nutritional foundation, self-discipline is second. All the knowledge in the world will not help you if you can't control your actions. You could know exactly what to eat and what not to eat, but if you don't have the discipline to incorporate that knowledge into your life, it will not help you.

Dictionary.com defines self-discipline as "disciplining or controlling of oneself or one's desires, actions, habits, etc."[43]

While knowledge can be gained by research and study, self-discipline is not something that can be acquired as easily. It takes time and perseverance. Self-discipline is built by winning small daily battles. Over time, these victories will condition you to be more disciplined in your life.

Gaining self-discipline at a young age will do wonders to help you live a long, healthy life. You can't teach an old dog new tricks. Not developing self-discipline now makes it even harder to develop later. Now is the time to start learning how to control your body. It's hard to resist the urge to eat what you shouldn't, especially at first. But the longer you go without doing so, the harder it will be to start.

> *Self-discipline is built by winning small daily battles.*

Eating Disorders

Eating becomes a disorder when a person's passion for thinness is overwhelming and out of control. It becomes an all consuming desire to the point that thinness is the number one priority in their life. The most common eating disorders are anorexia (starving oneself), and bulimia (binge-eating and "purging" by vomiting).

Eating disorders are a serious problem that affect over 8 million people in America alone.[44] Eighty-six percent of those with eating disorders say it started while they were a teenager.[45] One source suggests that as many as 20% of adolescents could be struggling with some form of an eating disorder.[44] Eating disorders affect the entire person: mind, body, and soul. They cause deep emotional and psychological scars. These disorders can cause permanent physical damage and can even become life-threatening.

Just look at the people on TV, the teenage divas, the singers, models, the actors and actresses. Be thin at all cost. That is the message they send. It seems to be a battle to be the boniest. These young people compromise their health in hopes that other people will approve of them. The sad thing about this illness is that often times, they still see themselves as overweight.

Some people become so consumed with their bodies that they are willing to do anything to make them look a certain way. Our culture's obsession with slenderness puts young people at a high risk for such behavior.

These disorders are powerful and addictive. Many of these people fool themselves into believing that they are controlling their lives by continuing the disorder, but in actuality, the disorder is controlling them.

Some of the long-term results of eating disorders include:

- Infertility (the inability to have children)
- Anemia (low iron in the blood causing extreme exhaustion)
- Osteoporosis (thinning of bones)
- Muscle deterioration
- Organ damage (kidneys, liver, heart, etc.)

- Acid reflux
- Brain shrinkage
- Stroke
- Heart attack
- Tearing of the esophagus
- Destruction of teeth enamel
- Death, if it is not treated[45]

If you are struggling with an eating disorder, it is very serious. Find an adult that you can trust to talk about these issues and help you overcome them.

Don't overlook your parents. Most parents of teenagers with eating disorders want to help. Let them know about it. Odds are they already do. Most parents will do everything they can to help you.

Be sure to let someone know you are struggling. It is too easy to become secretive about your problem and cut everyone else off. That will only hurt you.

If someone is pressuring you to look a certain way (a boyfriend or girlfriend, perhaps), then don't listen to them. Break up with them if they won't stop pressuring you! Find someone who will appreciate you for who you are.

Everyone is different. We all have different genes. You will never look just like someone else. But why would you want to? Individuality is what makes us beautiful. Learn to be happy in your own skin.

You can definitely overcome an eating disorder. It will be challenging, but people do it every day. You can do it too!

Teenage Construction Zone

Check out some helpful websites like:

www.AMAD.org

www.nationaleatingdisorders.org

www.mercyministries.com

HEALTH AND FITNESS
WEEK 10

Group Review

Last week, you came up with a plan to get help when you begin having suicidal thoughts. Share your plan with everyone else and take notes on any useful suggestions that someone else may have.

"The heart of the discerning acquires knowledge; the ears of the wise seek it out." (Proverbs 18:15)

1. According to this passage the discerning and the wise seek what? ______________________ When it comes to health and fitness, you need to seek out sources of good information. Look into how you should eat and how much you should exercise. Don't leave it up to your teachers or parents. Take it upon yourself.

Group Discussion

"Like a city whose walls are broken down is a man who lacks self-control." (Proverbs 25:28)

"It is God's will…that each of you should learn to control his own body in a way that is holy and honorable…" (1Thessalonians 4:3-4)

“For God did not give us a spirit of timidity, but a spirit of power, of love and of self-discipline.” (2 Timothy 1:7)

Why do you think the Bible has so much to say about self-control and self-discipline? How can God help?

____

____

2. Do you think it should be easier or more difficult for a Christian to maintain healthy habits when it comes to exercise and fitness? Why?

____

____

3. Everyone struggles with discipline at some time. What should we do when we are struggling? List at least two things that you could do spiritually.

1)____

____

2)____

____

List at least two things you could do practically (like get a friend to hold you accountable).

1)____

____

2)____

____

“Do you not know that your body is a temple of
the Holy Spirit, who is in you, whom you have
received from God? You are not your own; you
were bought at a price. Therefore honor God
with your body.” (1 Corinthians 6:19-20)

4. It is important to understand that you are not just taking care of your body for the sake of looking good. You are taking care of your body because it is actually _____'s property. The _________ is living in there with you!

Group Discussion

How does realizing that your body is the temple of God affect your decisions regarding health and exercise?

____

____

> "For physical training is of some value, but godliness has value for all things, holding promise for both the present life and the life to come." (1 Timothy 4:8)

5. Godliness comes first, but physical training is still of some value. What are you currently doing for exercise?

____

____

6. Set some realistic goals for your health and fitness. As this chapter stated, there are many ways to exercise and stay in shape. Find something that works for you. Take a moment and jot down some ideas that come to mind.

____

____

____

____

Exercise

Do something to change the healthiness of your lifestyle this week. Research some nutrition facts and apply them, change what you eat, and/or pick up and exercise routine if you don't already have one. Fulfill one of the goals you set for question 6 or start down the road to get there.

SEE NO EVIL, HEAR NO EVIL, SPEAK NO EVIL

CHAPTER 11

You've probably seen the old drawing before or heard the saying with the three monkeys. You know, the three wise monkeys. One monkey covering his eyes, the other monkey covering his ears, and the last covering his mouth.

While it might be a little difficult to take seriously, it's a great visual aid for how to live. The principles are very basic. Be careful of what you see, hear, or say.

If those simple guidelines are followed, they can do wonders to protect your foundation from bad choices. If we learn to try to block out the evil that is around us, instead of absorbing it, then we are far less likely to be affected by it. Establishing strong criteria in the areas of hearing no evil, seeing no evil, and speaking no evil in your life now can reap huge benefits later.

What? A Fourth Monkey?

I didn't draw the three monkeys, but if I did, I would have added one more: a monkey up above the others looking down at them to see what the other monkeys were going to do. I would name him the Thinking Monkey.

If we block out the evil that is around us, instead of absorbing it, then we are less likely to be affected by it.

What the other three monkeys do has a direct effect on the fourth, the Thinking Monkey. What you see, hear, and speak has a huge impact on your mind. That impact then plays a major role in what you allow yourself to see, hear and speak in the future.

Human beings don't do anything without thinking about it first. Your life reflects the thought processes of your mind. If a person can stop thinking about bad things, then they are far less likely to do bad things. Trying to change people's actions without changing their thinking only does a temporary, patchwork job. If you want to fix what you do, you must first fix how you think!

So what do you do to stop the insanity? Well, a person whose mind is filled with the right things does the right thing. Likewise, a person whose mind is filled with the wrong things does the wrong thing. That's why it's so important to keep high standards in what we say, hear and see. By doing so, we protect the most important one: the way we think.

All monkey business aside, your mind is the place in which the greatest battles of your life will be fought. The 4,000 choices you make a day are all made there. It is the place where you will process all the information that you receive. It is the place where you will decide every decision you make. As you begin to win the small battles that rage daily in your mind, victory in life will just be the natural result.

> *Your mind is the place in which the greatest battles of your life will be fought.*

What are your guidelines for what you think about? If you haven't considered it, then now is the time. "Whatever is true, whatever is noble, whatever is right, whatever is pure, whatever is lovely, whatever is admirable – if anything is excellent or praiseworthy – thinks about such things." Those are some great sample guidelines written by one wise dude over two thousand years ago.

Your life is under construction. The choices you make now will shape your entire future. It's more important now than ever to start controlling your thoughts.

See No Evil

Guard your eyes from seeing anything that could contaminate your mind. Once images are in your mind, they are very difficult to get out. Images are easily stored, and easily recalled. To this day I can easily recall scenes from a rated R movie that a friend and I snuck in to see while I was in the 7th grade.

What we see with our eyes is one of the main sources for forming our world view; what and how we think about moral issues. For example, it's hard to view sex as something that should be reserved for marriage when the average teenager sees over 14,000 sexual images a year through the media.[46] It's hard to view alcohol as something destructive, when there is a commercial for it every three minutes. It could become difficult to view life as precious when you see thousands of acts of violence and murder on your TV. Don't just let your eyes absorb whatever is on. Think critically. Is this a good influence on me or a bad one?

> *Once images are in your mind, they are difficult to get out.*

Television and Movies

What kind of movies are you watching? What kind of shows on TV do you follow? You may not think that what you watch affects you, but in actuality, it is one of the greatest influences on you and your life decisions. It is so easy to idealize a show or a person on a show and want to be like them. But TV paints a distorted view of reality. It's not real. I'm sorry to have to be the one to tell you this, but even reality shows are staged. Yet, it's pretty easy to use TV as a resource for how we act and interact in this world.

Internet

The internet is another avenue for quick contamination. When used the right way, the internet can be a great way to communicate, purchase, and find information. But used the wrong way, it can be a huge risk for seeing evil. For example, did you know that the vast majority of internet searches are for pornography?

To keep you from "seeing no evil" on the internet, intentionally or accidently, I suggest at least two barriers be enforced. First, allow someone else to put an adult content block on your computer that requires a password to get through. Second, make sure your computer is in a place where people could walk by any moment to glance at what you're looking at. These two little precautions can do wonders to keep evil away from your eyes.

Pornography

Pornography is more popular and easier to acquire then ever before. It's in magazines, on TV, and on the internet. Still, no matter how popular or accessible pornography is, it does not make it right. Pornography has nothing good or beneficial to offer anyone. When you take a young person already battling hormones and add pornography, you have a recipe for disaster.

Pornography is highly addictive. People who view somewhat milder pornographic images quickly want more extreme pornographic images. They become desensitized by what they are seeing and begin to crave more and more. Many crimes are connected to young men wanting to act out these fantasies, even when they do not have a willing partner. Pornography has been linked to rape, sexual violence, and sexual abuse.[47] Even when crimes are not committed by its viewers, countless relationships are destroyed.

Once exposed to pornography, it is more difficult for a person to have a realistic view of how sexuality in a marriage will actually be expressed. This can lead to much frustration. Sexual addictions can also occur. A person who views pornography can begin to try to satisfy that addiction with multiple partners. They're not looking for relationships, only sexual satisfaction. Accustomed to seeing so many nude images of many people, they quickly leave partners behind and move to someone else.[48]

Pornography is an extremely dangerous brick to put on anyone's foundation. As you construct your foundation during these critical years of your life, do yourself a favor and leave this one off!

Fries with that Shake?

> **The way you look at someone can quickly become wrong.**

Guys are notorious for staring at girls, lusting after girls, and looking at them as only sexual objects. The way you look at someone could become evil pretty quickly. Be careful how you look at people of the opposite sex. Your thoughts can turn south fast if you allow your eyes to stare too long. From one guy to the rest of you, try to train your eyes to look at females from the shoulders up. It's easy for guys to want to give girls the "up down" (looking them up and down as one high schooler put it), but do your best to avoid concentrating on the girls' bodies. It will only lead to frustration for you, and it demeans them.

> *How you dress says a lot about you. Are you saying good things or bad?*

On the opposite side of this matter girls, don't give them so much to look at. You don't have to wear revealing clothing to get guys to see you. Do you really want guys to like you just for your sexiness? I know that there is a lot more to you than that. You should know it too.

Trends come and go, but often times the trend for girls is to show as much of themselves as possible. It's usually one or more of the following: the lowest and tightest jeans, the shortest shorts, the lowest cut tops, or the tightest shirts. Many girls don't realize that guys are very visual creatures. Dressing sexy means more to a guy than it does to you. They often misinterpret revealing dress as a sign that you are willing to reveal even more. One of my mentors tells girls in high school, "If it's not for sale, then quit advertising it."

A little blunt, but it does drive the point home. How you dress says a lot about you. Do your best to dress in a way that fits your style but is not too revealing.

Hear No Evil

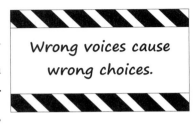

> **Wrong voices cause wrong choices.**

What we hear each day plays an important role in who we become. Zig Ziglar puts it best when he says, "Input determines outlook, and outlook determines our outcome."[49]

Guard your ears from hearing anything that is negative. I understand that truly allowing no evil into your ears might mean that you need to wear ear plugs all day long. While that might work, it probably wouldn't sit well with your teachers or parents.

Instead, make every effort to avoid listening to any negative messages that come from gossip, cursing, putdowns, and negative song lyrics. The last thing you need during these foundational years is one more voice encouraging you to make a bad decision. Wrong voices can cause wrong choices.

Gossip

"You won't believe what I heard about ______!" A little bit of truth, a little bit of un-truth, mix it all up, and voila! You've got gossip. Gossip is very common amongst teens and adults alike. It's also very destructive.

Gossip is often used to belittle someone else, to destroy a person's reputation, to spread a lie, or just to make the gossiper feel better about themselves. It's not just innocent fun, it is cruel and destructive. Virtually all gossip is damaging to someone.

It's hard to stop a piece of gossip because there is something about it that makes us want to hear it. Whole magazines and TV shows are built on providing people with juicy gossip about Hollywood stars. It might be somewhat enjoyable, but it is still wrong.

Gossip is usually never verified by its hearers to see if it is true, so the lies keep spreading, growing further and further from the truth.

Have you ever played the gossip game with a large group of people? Everyone sits in a circle. One person is given a sentence to whisper to the person to their right. Then that person has to tell the sentence to the person on their right. You can only say the sentence one time to them. This process is repeated until it comes all the way back around.

Gossip gets further and further away from the truth every time it is told.

By the time the sentence works its way back around, it's amazing how the sentence will have totally changed. The more people involved, the further from the original sentence they get. You might start with "red raspberries are good to eat," but by the twentieth person, the sentence will be "I've got reindeer on my feet." That is exactly how gossip works in real life as well. It gets further and further from the truth every time it is told.

How do you stop it? You can't control others from gossiping, but you can at least stop it from spreading through you. Don't even be a listening ear to those who enjoy gossiping.

Most people see nothing wrong with it. By showing that you aren't going to participate in it, odds are others will give a little more thought to just how wrong gossip can actually be.

If you have been a victim of gossip, then what should you do? You should make the truth known. However, don't feel that you have to try to find everyone and get the truth to them. You'll never get to everyone, and you'll become more and more bitter the longer you have to deal with it.

Let your closest few friends know the truth and then drop the matter completely. Don't retaliate with creating more gossip or the cycle will continue. But most importantly, live your life in such a way that people who hear the gossip will not believe it because they know that the story does not fit your character.

Music

Music is another way for our ears to be receivers of evil. While music itself is not bad, sometimes the lyrics that accompany it can be subtly, or even outright, evil. George Barna, in his book *Real Teens*, states, "For millions of young people, music produces a life philosophy for them to consider and follow; cultural heroes and role models to look up to and imitate; values and lifestyles to embrace."[50]

See No Evil, Hear No Evil, Speak No Evil

Music is not just music. Many young people use it as a valuable source of information to determine how they live their lives. Even if you don't think that you are letting music affect you, you may be surprised at what effect it has on your subconscious.

Don't fool yourself into thinking that songs don't affect you. When you hear the same message over and over, there is going to be an effect.

Ever had a song stuck in your head for a whole day? Everyone has. But have you ever had a math problem stuck in your head all day? Probably not. There is something powerful about words mixed with music that make them easy to memorize, even if the message is bad.

Sometimes we forget that the entertainment industry is a business. They make music to sell, not to do what's best for you. Songs that encourage low moral standards or promote premarital sex, violence, drugs, and alcohol often soar to the top on popularity charts. Does that mean that it's okay for you to listen to them? No!

Choose music that stylistically fits you, yet does not compromise what you stand for.

You shouldn't stop listening to music but you should be selective. Being selective doesn't mean just buying the same music with the bad language removed. In all honesty, that accomplishes nothing. You can easily make out what word the artist is using and fill it in with your mind every time you hear it. More importantly, songs that have bad language generally also have immoral or negative messages that you don't want to allow into your mind. Try to choose music that stylistically fits you, yet does not compromise what you stand for.

One of the biggest mistakes people make is just listening to whatever is popular. Anytime you use popularity as your only criteria, you're asking for trouble. Think for yourself. You're not like everyone else. You have higher standards in your choices, in what you let in your body, how you date, and yes, even what you listen to.

A simple test when choosing music is to ask yourself: "If the lyrics of this song were applied to my life, would they be beneficial?"

> A simple test to pick music is to ask yourself: If the lyrics were applied to my life, would it be beneficial?

Be honest. I challenge you to take a critical look at what music you already have. Do you need to delete some songs or throw some CD's away? Remember, what you hear changes the way you think and act.

Speak No Evil

"Sticks and stones may break my bones, but words will never hurt me." This old saying, while used by many well intended 2nd graders to thwart bullies, is simply not true.

While words may not break bones, they do have the power to break someone's heart. Cussing, verbal bullying, put downs, and gossiping are all ways that people allow evil to come out of their mouths.

Your words are powerful. Everyone has been hurt by someone's carless words. I remember in the 9th grade, I was on the bus looking out the window, and out of nowhere this nice looking girl in front of me turns around to say something.

> **Words may not break bones, but they do break hearts.**

I looked up in anticipation, just to hear her say, "Man, you've got a big ol' head."

Wow, what was I supposed to think about that? It's not like I could change it. It's my head. I'm kind of stuck with it.

I remember the insecurity her one sentence caused. She immediately went back to talking to her friends, but I was consumed by what she said for the rest of the day.

How powerful were her words? Well, twenty years later, I can still remember them perfectly. I can even visualize them coming out of her mouth. I can't remember verbatim anything anyone else told me that year, but I remember that one careless put down.

Years later, I finally just accepted that, yeah, I actually do have a pretty big noggin, but I just tell people it's that way to fit around my big brain. Those who know me think that's pretty funny.

Most people don't realize just how powerful their words are. One cruel word towards someone, especially a young person, has the power to drastically affect them for years to come. Your words have the power to discourage, but they also have the power to motivate.

> ***Most people don't realize how powerful their words are.***

Well meant words from a sincere heart can bring comfort and reassurance. Your words have the power to heal people, to make them forgive, and to make them understand. The words that we speak change our lives and the lives of those around us.

There was an ancient writer that wrote a lot about wisdom and speech. These standards that the author was trying to apply to his life so long ago are still very applicable to us today. Here are just a few samples:

"He who guards his lips guards his soul, but he who speaks rashly will come to ruin."

"He who holds his tongue is wise."

"The lips of the wise nourish many."

What if everyone knew the full impact of the words that they were speaking? The world would be a different place, that's for sure. What if you become a positive verbal force to be reckoned with at home, at school, and with your friends? What would happen to your world?

I had a teacher in high school that could motivate like no

teacher I have ever had. Mr. Blackwell, the FFA instructor, got me to do things I never thought I would do. Out of nowhere, he told me to deliver a speech to our entire high school.

I thought he was crazy. Who did he think I was? I was just a freshmen, and I had never done anything like that before. No way was I going to give a speech in from of the entire school!

Two weeks later, guess what I was doing? You guessed it, giving a speech in front of the entire school. I did horribly! It was one of the most embarrassing moments of my entire life. I forgot the words and just stared at all the people.

Mr. Blackwell just encouraged me even more. By the time I was in the 10th grade, I was competing in speaking competitions around the state. Today, I have a career in motivational speaking. Now that's an example of the power that words have to motivate.

Become an encourager, not a discourager. Be known as someone who lifts others up, not someone who puts them down. People love positive people. They are magnets to success and their friendship is greatly desired. One of the smallest but most powerful things you will ever try to control on this planet is your tongue. Use it to bring about good, not evil.

> *Be known as someone who lifts others up, not someone who puts them down.*

How the Weak Speak

Around middle school, some teens usually start thinking

that using cuss words is pretty cool. By now you've been around them, or maybe you're even one of them.

Cussing reveals so much about a person. If I am around someone who is cussing, I can immediately assume with pretty good accuracy that that person doesn't have good standards in most areas of their life.

People who habitually cuss look like they're somewhat lacking in the area of IQ. Instead of exercising their brain to find the right descriptive word, they'll just use a cuss word as a filler.

Cussing also reveals that that person is probably struggling with insecurity. They cuss to appear tough on the outside, but they are actually weak on the inside.

As you can see, cussing is not something that I enjoy. In fact, in college, I got so sick of it that I wouldn't let anyone cuss once they entered my room. Before long, people caught on, and I finally had a little safe haven from having to listen to it. There is just no need to cuss. You can communicate better without it, it proves nothing, and it definitely doesn't make you tough.

Do you use four letter words yourself? Why? Maybe you've never given much thought to it. Maybe you've allowed others' bad speaking habits to rub off on you. It's always good to know what you're doing and why you're doing it. And cussing is no exception.

Expect more from yourself and those that you hang around with.

No More Monkeys

You know what the monkeys mean now. You know how seeing no evil, hearing no evil, and speaking no evil relate to the new monkey, thinking no evil. Now it's up to you to determine how you are going to handle these four wise monkeys. How much evil are you going to allow into your life?

What I'm saying is a big deal. The choices that you are placing on your foundation are constantly being influenced by what you think, see, hear, or speak. The quality of your entire life will depend on how you handle these wise monkeys. Tame them before they tame you. Choose to have a great life.

SEE NO EVIL, HEAR NO EVIL, SPEAK NO EVIL
WEEK 11

Group Review

Last week's lesson was about health and fitness. Why is it important to maintain our health as a Christian?

"I made a covenant with my eyes not to look lustfully at a girl." (Job 31:1)

1. Is it acceptable in our society to look but not touch?

2. Is it acceptable for you as a Christian to look but not touch?

3. What are some ways to keep yourself from looking at evil on the internet?

"The tongue has the power of life and death." (Proverbs 18:21a)

4. Think about what you talk about on a daily basis. Are your words helping or hurting the people around you?

"Let the word of Christ dwell in you richly as you teach and admonish one another with all wisdom, and as you sing psalms, hymns and spiritual songs with gratitude in your hearts to God." (Colossians 3:16)

5. What must dwell in us if we are to help others with the words of our mouths? ____________________. How do we increase the word of God that is in our minds and hearts?

____

____

Group Discussion

"Nor should there be obscenity, foolish talk or coarse joking, which are out of place, but rather thanksgiving." (Ephesians 5:4)

What is "coarse joking" and how could coarse joking hurt someone's feelings? Think of examples in your own life, or others, where someone has joked too harshly resulting in someone getting hurt.

"Avoid godless chatter, because those who indulge in it will become more and more ungodly." (2 Timothy 2:16)

6. Give some examples of "godless chatter."

____

____

"A gossip betrays a confidence; so avoid a man who talks too much." (Proverbs 20:19)

7. How do you deal with someone who gossips too much?

"Do not let any unwholesome talk come out of your mouths, but only what is helpful for building others up according to their needs, that it may benefit those who listen." (Ephesians 4:29)

"The Lord detests the thoughts of the wicked, but those of the pure are pleasing to him." (Proverbs 15:26)

"Finally, brothers, whatever is true, whatever is noble, whatever is right, whatever is pure, whatever is lovely, whatever is admirable--if anything is excellent or praiseworthy--think about such things." (Philippians 4:8)

8. The Bible gives us strict commands about what we are supposed to think about. If it is not noble, __________, pure, _______, admirable, ____________, or praiseworthy, then don't allow it in your brain.

9. What are some things that interfere with you keeping your thoughts fixed on Jesus?

Group Discussion

What are some practical standards you can apply to these three areas of your life.

See?

Hear?

Say?

Exercise

This week be more observant of what you are watching, listening to, or saying. Identify potential problem areas and take steps to change.

WORTH THE WORK

CHAPTER 12

Alex had built houses for over forty years. His job was to oversee the construction of every project that his company undertook. This included everything from homes and apartments to large commercial buildings.

Alex enjoyed what he did. He liked the work and the position that he had earned over the years. Still, Alex had just one problem. He had always thought that he deserved more money. Now, he was getting ready to retire in less than a year, and he wasn't sure if he had enough money set aside for him and his family.

His boss was well aware that Alex was about to retire, so he asked Alex to take on one last big project. The boss told him that he needed a grand home built. The home would be bigger and better than anything else they had done in the past. He gave Alex the details of the project and told him to construct a house that was built for a king.

Even Alex was surprised by the magnitude of the project. The house was to be 4,000 square feet with six bedrooms, an in home theatre, a game room, five bathrooms, an office, and a four car garage. The boss had told him to spare nothing and to use only the finest building materials possible for the construction.

Alex nicknamed the project "the King's Palace." He started work just as he had done thousands of times before, but this time, there was something different.

He grew more and more frustrated with the thought of his low salary over the last 40 years. He began to think about all of his hard work, the long days, and his complete oversight of all the company's projects. The more he thought about his approaching retirement and how much money he needed, the more bitter he became.

He decided that for this last project, he would choose building materials that were not the highest quality and to pocket the money that he saved (which is illegal, by the way).

Construction on the King's Palace was now underway. The foundation of the house was poured faster than usual and not even cured properly to save money. The 2x4's used to frame the house were the cheapest, lowest quality he could find. Instead of buying the roofing shingles that would last twenty years, he just bought the ones that had a 2 year warranty on them. To the untrained eye, the palace still looked like it was fit for a king, but Alex knew what it truly was.

Alex called his boss one night and told him that the King's

Palace was finally complete. The boss flew in the next day to see the finished work and to celebrate Alex's retirement. That night Alex, his wife, the boss and several other employees dined at very nice restaurant in honor of Alex's retirement.

At the end of the night, the boss stood up and began to thank Alex for all of his years of dedicated service to the company. He thanked him over and over again. He said that he had always wanted to pay him more but couldn't and thanked him for staying anyway.

Then the boss reached into his pocket and pulled out a set of keys. He held the keys in front of him and said,

"Alex, I know that you have been stressed out about retirement and providing for your family. I cannot thank you enough for what you have done for us over the years. I want you to know that the project you have been working on this year is not for one of our clients. It was for me to give back to you. The reason I wanted it built so perfectly, is because you deserve every bit of it! The King's Palace is all yours!"

On the outside Alex smiled and accepted the great gift, but on the inside he was appalled. If he had built the home like he was supposed to, it would have been the house of his dreams. It would have been virtually indestructible. Now, it was a disaster waiting to happen.

Many of us, like Alex, are unaware that we are working on and constructing the most important project ever: our lives. Some people think that they can take shortcuts, use inferior products, and still build a palace fit for a king. They are only deceiving themselves. Sooner or later, the quality of their building will be shown for what it is. Only those who work hard to do what's right will one day be able to enjoy the fruit of their labor in a palace fit for a king.

> *You are constructing the most important project ever: your life.*

The keys Alex was handed that day were actually his all along, even though he didn't know it. But you do. You are the general contractor and the keys you hold are to your own life. What you build is up to you!

Foundation Inspection

If you have read this book and honestly believe that you are building the best foundation you possibly can in every area of your life, then keep up the good work. You will reap the benefits for the rest of your life.

However, the odds are that during the course of reading this book, you came across something that you realized is or could be a weakness in your foundation. I have never met a perfect person. There is always room for improvement.

I don't say that to let anyone off the hook, but to let you know that we all have places in our lives that need some work. The key is not to ignore, deny, or excuse your problems, but to work on them.

If you have realized that you are placing bad choices on your foundation, stop immediately! If engineers determined that the foundation to a building was too weak, they would stop all construction, analyze the problem, and make the adjustments to fix the problem. I challenge you to do the same. Stop everything, analyze what's wrong, and focus your attention on fixing the problem before you go any further with your foundation.

Maybe you need to try harder in school. Maybe you need to correct some bad habits that you have already formed. Maybe you need to change friends. Maybe you need to evaluate if you should really be in that relationship. Maybe you need to change where you hang out after school. Maybe you need to get help for a drug addiction. Maybe you need to stop letting negative things like gossip and cursing come out of your mouth.

Whatever your diagnosis is, fix it. I promise that you will never regret adding strength to your foundation.

I have talked to many teens that have made bad choices and feel like it is too late for them. Although it may be more difficult, it's still worth it to make positive changes. This isn't just your life we are talking about. It is your future, your eventual spouse's future, and your children's future. This affects everyone around you.

I know there are times when you might wish that you could go back and erase some of your past mistakes, but that's impossible. While the pages of your past are already written, the pages of your future are totally blank. Learn from your past mistakes but don't dwell on them. Concentrate on improving what happens next.

There is a saying: "No one is born a winner. No one is born a loser. But we are all born choosers."

If you want to be a winner in life, then start making winning choices today! You are what you choose to be. The quality of your life is determined by the choices that you are making every day. You are in charge of the construction of your life, so build wisely!

The Beginning

Even though this is the last chapter of the book, try to think of it as the beginning. The beginning of a great future. If you can get through these critical years of your life and avoid putting these major mistakes in your foundation, then you will find it far easier to come out a winner in every area. You will avoid the addictions, the baggage, and the physical, mental, and emotional setbacks that so many people have to deal with. You will accomplish a huge victory.

It's going to be hard, but the most rewarding things in life are the things that we work for the hardest. I congratulate you on the strong foundation that I know you will build for yourself!

While the pages of your past are already written, the pages of your future are totally blank.

WORTH THE WORK
WEEK 12

Group Review

Why is it important to guard what we see, hear, and say? What was the fourth monkey that I added and why is it important?

> "Not that I have already obtained all this, or have already been made perfect, but I press on to take hold of that for which Christ Jesus took hold of me." (Philippians 3:12)

1. In this life, can you ever get to a point where you are absolutely perfect? Explain.

2. Paul, the person who wrote these verses, had a horrible past, but an amazing future. He went on to write two thirds of the New Testament. Do you think "forgetting what is behind and straining toward what is ahead" was very important to him? How and why should this be an important principle or your life?

"Commit to the Lord whatever you do, and your plans will succeed." (Proverbs 16:3)

"And whatever you do, whether in word or deed, do it all in the name of the Lord Jesus, giving thanks to God the Father through him." (Colossians 3:17)

3. Whether its athletics, band, walking down the hallway, homework, talking to friends, or anything else, you should do it all in the name of __________.

You are not just representing yourself, you are representing Jesus. Strive for excellence in every part of your life as if you were doing it not just for a coach, parents, teachers, or friends, but for Jesus himself.

"How can a young man keep his way pure? By living according to your word. I seek you with all my heart; do not let me stray from your commands. I have hidden your word in my heart that I might not sin against you. Praise be to you, O LORD; teach me your decrees. With my lips I recount all the laws that come from your mouth. I rejoice in following your statutes as one rejoices in great riches. I meditate on your precepts and consider your ways. I delight in your decrees; I will not neglect your word." (Psalms 119:9-16)

4. I like to call this passage "The Cure to Stay Pure." The writer looks at the evil all around him and says, "How can a young man keep his way pure?" We could easily ask the same question today. We could also answer it the same. What was his answer to his question?

5. How can you live the word if you don't know the word, and how can you know the word if you don't read the word! Write down the last part of the last sentence of the verse above.

I ______ not__________ your __________.

6. Consulting God's word is something that we should do on a daily basis. When was the last time you read your Bible?

Group Discussion

What are some practical things that we can do to keep from neglecting Gods word, so that we can live a pure life?

"Run in such a way as to get the prize. Everyone who competes in the games goes into strict training. They do it to get a crown that will not last; but we do it to get a crown that will last forever. Therefore I do not run like a man running aimlessly; I do not fight like a man beating the air." (1 Corinthians 9:24b-25)

8. Live with purpose and intentionality. Your purpose is to bring God glory through your life. In the end that is all that is going to matter. This life is temporary, but eternity is forever. Make sure your working for a ___________ that lasts.

Group Discussion

In the section Foundation Inspection you are challenged to truly examine your foundation thus far. Do you think this type of inspection is common amongst teenagers? Why or why not? Do you believe that it should become an important part of your life?

____

____

Exercise

What you build is up to you! Spend some time this week looking back over some paragraphs in the book that really applied to you. Also look back over your Goal Exercise and this workbook. The best way to get something in your head is through repetition. Review and apply.

SALVATION

Question: Where do you stand with God?

Answer:

ⓐ I don't know.

ⓑ Heaven, baby!

ⓒ I'm pretty skeptical about that whole thing.

The Bible says that you are either on the road to Heaven or the road to Hell. There are no other choices. But how do you know which road you are on? Lets look up verses from the book of Romans to find out.

> "For all have sinned and fall short of the glory of God." (Romans 3:23)

> "For the wages of sin is death, but the gift of God is eternal life in Christ Jesus our Lord." (Romans 6:23)

First, it is important to realize that we are all sinners. If you are a human, then you are a sinner. It's that simple.

The punishment for sin is death. And this doesn't mean that you stop breathing. No, this death means that we are spending our life on Earth without God and our life after Earth - all eternity - in Hell.

Fortunately, Jesus is the Son of God. He was perfect from birth, and He lived a perfect life. Therefore, he could pay the price for our sin, a price that we could never pay ourselves.

"But God demonstrates his own love for us in this: While we were still sinners, Christ died for us." (Romans 5:8)

God knows you have sinned. In fact, He knows every sin you have ever committed, but He is willing to forgive you. You can call on Him by faith, and He will save you from your sins and the death that you deserve. You can have an eternal life in heaven instead.

"That if you confess with your mouth, 'Jesus is Lord,' and believe in your heart that God raised him from the dead, you will be saved." (Romans 10:9)

"Everyone who calls on the name of the Lord will be saved." (Romans 10:13)

If you would like to receive God's gift of eternal life, you may want to voice a prayer like the one below.

"Dear Jesus,

Thank you for living, dying, and rising from the dead so that I could be saved. You are God, and I know that I have sinned against you. Thank you for allowing me to see my sin and the need for you as my Savior. I receive your salvation and forgiveness of sin. Thank you for making me a child of God."

Congratulations, if you have believed what we have just gone over, then you are saved! What does the book of Romans have to say about you now?

"Therefore, there is now no condemnation for those who are in Christ Jesus." (Romans 8:1)

"Since we have now been justified by his blood, how much more shall we be saved from God's wrath through him!" (Romans 5:9)

Salvation

That's right, your sins are forgiven. Jesus saved you from an eternity in Hell, separated from God.

> "For I am convinced that neither death nor life, neither angels nor demons, neither the present nor the future, nor any powers, neither height nor depth, nor anything else in all creation, will be able to separate us from the love of God that is in Christ Jesus our Lord." (Romans 8:38-39)

Once you are saved, your sins are totally forgiven, you are a child of God. Let someone know about your salvation! Don't keep the greatest news in your life a secret.

Endnotes

1. Swindoll, Charles. Attitudes: The Power of a Positive Outlook. Grand Rapids: Zondervan, 1995.

2. Chesterton, Gilbert Keith. Illustrated London News 5 May 1928.

3. Bok, Sissela. Lying : Moral Choice in Public and Private Life. New York: Vintage Books, 2002.

4. Too Much…Too Fast…Can Kill You. Del Mar, CA: San Dieguito Alliance for Drug Free Youth. Winter 2008 <http://www.sandieguitoalliance.org>.

5. Sandars, Bill. Tough Turf: A Teen Survival Manual. Old Tappen, NJ: Revell, 1986. 152.

6. 11 Shocking Facts about Teens and Drug Use. Do Something. Fall 2008. <http://www.dosomething.org/tipsandtools/11-shocking-facts-about-teens-and-drug-use>.

7. Greenblatt, Janet. "Patterns of Alcohol Use among Adolescents and Associations with Emotional and Behavioral Problems." Substance Abuse and Mental Health Services Administration. Mar. 2000. Substance Abuse and Mental Health Services Administration 12 Mar. 2009 <http://www.oas.samhsa.gov/NHSDA/TeenAlc/teenalc.pdf>.

8. Shalala, Donna E. "Alcohol Alert." National Institute on Alcohol Abuse and Alcoholism. Oct. 2000. National Institute on Alcohol Abuse and Alcoholism. 12 Mar. 2009 <http://pubs.niaaa.nih.gov/publications/aa29.htm>.

9. Parrott, Les, and Leslie Parrott. Helping the Struggling Adolescent : A Guide to Thirty-Six Common Problems for Counselors, Pastors, and Youth Workers. Grand Rapids: Zondervan, 2000.

10. See note 7.

11. See note 8.

12. See note 3.

13. Prevent Peer Pressure. Winter 2008 <http://www.preventpeer-pressure.com>.

14. "Tobacco Use: Targeting the Nation's Leading Killer." Department of Health and Human Services Centers for Disease Control and Prevention. Jan. 2009. CDC. 12 Mar. 2009 <http://www.cdc.gov/NCCDPHP/publications/aag/osh.htm>.

15. "Research Report Series: Marijuana Abuse." National Institute on Drug Abuse. October 2001 National Institute on Drug Abuse. 12 Mar. 2009 <http://www.drugabuse.gov/ResearchReports/marijuana/default.html>.

16. Sexually transmitted Diseases." Life Wisconsin Right to Life. 2008. Wisconsin Right to Life. 12 Mar. 2009 <http://www.wrtl.org/sexandpregnancy/sexuallytransmitteddiseases.aspx>.

17. Swierziwitsky, Stanley."Teen Pregnancy." Women's Health Channel. 1 Mar. 2009. <http://www.womenshealthchannel.com/teenpregnancy/index.shtml>.

18. See note 8.

19. Horn, Wade F. and Tom Sylvester. Father Facts, 4th ed. Gaithersburg, MD: National Fatherhood Initiative, 2002. 15.

20. See note 8.

21. See note 8.

22. McPherson, Miles. I Don't Want Your Sex for Now. New York: Bethany House, 2001.

23. Ankerberg, John and John Weldon. The Facts on Abortion. Eugene, OR: Harvest House Publishers, 1995.

24. Dobson, James C. Life on the Edge : A Young Adult's Guide to a Meaningful Future. Danbury: Thomas Nelson Inc., 1995.

25. Staso, Paul. "Little Known Fitness/Health Facts." P.A.C.E. Trek. 2008. P.A.C.E. 12 Mar. 2009 <http://www.pacetrek.com/statistics.htm>.

26. Doyle, J. Andrew. "The Benefits of Exercise." The Exercise and Physical Fitness Page. Nov. 1997. Department of Kinesiology and Health at Georgia State University. 03 Jan 2009 <http://www2.gsu.edu/~wwwfit/benefits.html>.

27. See note 26.

28. See note 26.

29. See note 26.

30. See note 26.

31. See note 26.

32. See note 26.

33. See note 26.

34. Mayo Clinic Staff. "Exercise7: Benefits of Regular Physical Activity." Mayo Clinic Medical Information and Tools for Healthy Living. July 2007. Mayo Foundation for Medical Education and Research. 03 Jan 2009 <http://WWW.MAYO-CLINIC.COM>.

35. See note 34.

36. See note 34.

37. "The Human Brain - Exercise." The Franklin Institute. The Franklin Institute. 11 Mar. 2009 <http://www.fi.edu/learn/brain/exercise.html>.

38. See note 34.

39. NIDDK. "Take Charge of Your Health! A Guide for Teenagers." Weight Control Information Network. 2006. NIDDK. 12 Mar. 2009 <http://www.win.niddk.nih.gov/publications/take_charge.htm>.

40. See note 39.

41. "Self-Discipline." Dictionary.com Unabridged (v 1.1). Random House, Inc. 11 Mar. 2009. <Dictionary.com http://dictionary.reference.com/browse/self-discipline>.

42. "Facts about Eating Disorders." National Association of Anorexia Nervosa and Associated Eating Disorders. 3 Jan. 2009 National Association of Anorexia Nervosa and Associated Eating Disorders. 12 Mar. 2009 < http://www.anad.org/22385/index.html>.

43. See note 42.

44. See note 8.

45. Alcorn, Nancy. Starved : Mercy for Eating Disorders. Grand Rapids: WinePress, 2007.

46. Klepacki, Linda. "What Your Teens Need to Know about Sex." Focus On The Family. 2005. Focus on the Family. Feb 2008 <http://www.focusonthefamily.com/lifechallenges/love_and_sex/purity/what_your_teens_need_to_know_about_sex.aspx>.

47. See note 8.

48. "Teen Sexual Behavior Issues and Concerns." Focus Adolescent Services. Focus Adolescent Services. 12 Mar. 2009 <http://www.focusas.com/SexualBehavior.html>.

49. Ziglar, Zig, comp. Breaking Through to the Next Level. Tulsa: Honor Books, 1998.

50. Barna, George. Real Teens. New York: Regal Books, 2001.